They Tell of Birds

Chaucer
Spenser
Milton
Drayton

Army Medical Library, Cleveland, Ohio

The first illustration of birds in a printed book. (From Johann von Cube, *Hortus Sanitatis,* printed by Jacob Meydenbach, Mainz, 1491.)

They Tell of Birds

Chaucer
Spenser
Milton
Drayton

By THOMAS P. HARRISON

GREENWOOD PRESS, PUBLISHERS
WESTPORT, CONNECTICUT

First Greenwood Reprinting 1969

Library of Congress Catalogue Card Number 71-90523

SBN 8371-2779-3

PRINTED IN UNITED STATES OF AMERICA

"To THE ORNAMENT of the ayre bylongen byrdes and foules as Beda sayth. And therfore by the helpe of the goodnes of Jhusu Cryst som what of them shall be treated consequently in this boke." (*Bartholomeus de proprietatibus rerum,* translated by Trevisa and printed by Wynken de Worde, 1495)

Preface

THESE STUDIES OF BIRDS IN POETRY were undertaken with three purposes in mind. From one point of view the book comprises a series of separate studies in four poets, each chapter an intensive survey of allusions to birds in the individual's work. Birds—local and otherwise—their habits, their natures as emblems of human behavior—such is the matter of poetic allusion; and effort is made to explain these aspects of bird lore in terms of the poet's reading or direct observation. Prose antecedents are freely quoted, not as "sources" but as exemplars of a tradition. Emphasis is upon the nature and the origins of poetic allusion to birds. To a lesser extent I have endeavored also to show how allusions to birds are adapted to artistic purpose, as, for instance, in Spenser's similes drawn from falconry. Each chapter follows generally the chronology of composition, so that it is possible to learn something about the development of the poet's manner of introducing birds. In Chaucer and in Drayton this artistic evolution may clearly be observed.

But these chapters may be regarded as more than separate inquiries in so far as they provide a new basis of comparison for four poets whose work is closely linked on grounds remote from natural history. Spenser acknowledged Chaucer as his "Tityrus," Milton everywhere showed his reverence for "our sage and serious Spenser," and with all three Drayton's poetry was closely knit. It would be superfluous to dwell here upon the generally recognized aspects of this poetic kinship. The extent of their knowledge of birds, the tradition with which each poet is aligned, their different uses of the same birds, such as nightingale and cuckoo—not only are these inquiries individually interesting, but taken together they have significant bearing upon the attitudes of these poets to the natural world, as also upon their differing habits of adapting natural history to poetic uses.

Inevitably these considerations lead to the larger question of the relation of this group of poets to the scientific movement. It is a commonplace that Renaissance science was marked by increasingly objective study of nature as opposed to reliance upon authority. The new impulse was apparent in the waning popularity of the encyclopedia and more explicitly in the appearance of critical studies of Aristotle; in ornithology Turner, Belon, and Gesner were ultimately to replace Physiologus and Bartholomew. Within a restricted area of natural history this book explores the ways in which poetry was touched by this current of change. Spenser and Milton, it appears, tend to perpetuate the tradition of bestiary and encyclopedia—both their matter and their underlying philosophy; Chaucer anticipates, and Drayton shares, the spirit of the new science. This thesis is suggested only within narrow limits, for birds are but one phenomenon of the natural world and four poets scarcely represent with entire fairness the three centuries in which they lived. As a whole, then, these studies constitute a somewhat tentative chapter in the relations of poetry and science at a crucial period in the history of thought. This relationship is more intelligible after a review of some representative figures belonging to the centuries immediately preceding the new awakening in science. Chapter I attempts to provide this need and, as an addendum, to illustrate medieval poetic conventions which involved the introduction of birds.

The exclusion of Shakespeare from this study has seemed desirable for two reasons. In the first place, as dramatist Shakespeare was beyond the reach of those influences which guided the poetic tradition from Chaucer through Drayton; and to concentrate upon the natural sequence of this quartet is a major objective of this book. Furthermore, in his own province as the dramatist unique in his habits of introducing the lore of nature, Shakespeare has been explored by several students: J. E. Harting (1871), Thistelton Dyer (1883), H. W. Seager (1896), and Sir Archibald Geike (1916), to name the best known. Shakespeare's allusions to birds, as to all natural phenomena, are invariably striking "in the marvellous power of embellishing his ideas by the most apposite illustrations," as Dyer remarks. But this unique gift has often been mistaken for exactness of observation, which in the plant world is more apparent than in that of birds. For his bird lore Shakespeare leans heavily upon legend. In powers of observation and in breadth of knowledge of birds Drayton may well be considered Shakespeare's superior.

Obviously this book is intended primarily for students of literature. But aside from purely literary considerations, subsequent chapters should hold some interest for the ornithologist. Throughout the discussions, the author has given the modern bird names beside the old. The index of bird names at the end of the book comprises a complete list of all bird allusions of the poets in question, thus indicating the directions of interest for each member of the group. With the aid of cross reference it may also serve as a guide to prior discussion of individual birds and to quotations more extensive than those few in the Index. All in all, the bird student will find that even this small area of investigation further bears out the observation of the distinguished British ornithologist E. M. Nicholson: "We owe to poets a wealth of records of living wild birds in periods long before scientific ornithology had started."

It remains to record my obligations. The chapter on Drayton, somewhat revised, appeared first in the *University of Texas Studies in English*.[1] For permission to include this essay in revised form, I am obliged to the editor of this publication. For assistance in the scattered translations from Latin texts, I am obliged to Professors Oscar W. Reinmuth and Harry J. Leon of the Department of Classical Languages, University of Texas. The completed manuscript of the book was read by Dr. Giles E. Dawson of the Folger Shakespeare Library and by the Reverend Edward A. Armstrong of Cambridge, England. To both these gentlemen I am most grateful. In revising, I have had the full benefit of their advice in matters both great and small. I remember the kindnesses of untold library officials

[1] Vol. XXIX (1950), 102–17.

both in America and in England, but especially the intelligent help of Miss Kathleen Blow, Reference Librarian at the University of Texas. Gratitude is due also to Mr. W. B. Alexander for my cordial reception at the Edward Grey Institute at Oxford and to Mr. Philip Brown of the Royal Society for the Protection of Birds, in London. Access to the unique Alexander Library and permission to visit bird sanctuaries throughout England enabled me to combine the advantages of books with those of field work. Finally, I wish to acknowledge grants from the Research Council of the University of Texas both in extending to me a leave of absence during the spring of 1953 and in authorizing a partial subsidy which helped make possible the publication of this book.

THOMAS P. HARRISON

Austin, Texas
June, 1956

Contents

Illustrations

They Tell of Birds

Chaucer
Spenser
Milton
Drayton

I : *The Background*

Science

To the study of all branches of natural history Aristotle applied the method of direct observation of living creatures. In this lies the secret of his vast contributions, some of which have carried over virtually unaltered into modern times. "When he treats of Natural History," remarks D'Arcy Thompson, "his language is our language, and his methods and his problems are wellnigh identical with our own. He had familiar knowledge of a thousand varied forms of life, of bird and beast, and plant and creeping things."[1]

Aristotle described about 170 birds, though by no means have all of these been satisfactorily identified.[2] Some two thousand years later, with the first critical study of Aristotle, the major problem was to identify the Greek birds in terms of actual birds known in the field and named in the various vernaculars. In this task, it will be seen, the English Turner (d. 1568) was an important pioneer. With modifications Aristotle's sixfold classification of birds according to their food was repeated through the centuries, and in modern times has proved useful (on Chaucer see page 35). Where he was unable to confirm or deny, Aristotle freely admitted into his writings popular beliefs handed down the centuries. For example, he repeated the traditional theory that the sea eagle (*Haliaetus*) kills those of its young which are unable to gaze upon the sun.[3] Further examples of such fallacies appear in his theories concerning the transmutation of species and hibernation. Included along with the more solid results of direct observation, such beliefs were long perpetuated until, with more fruitful incentives, Turner and others of his complexion were able to produce accurate data from the field.

The chief concern of the present inquiry being poets and their knowledge of birds and bird lore, it is interesting to

[1] *On Aristotle as a Biologist,* the Herbert Spencer Lecture (Oxford, Clarendon Press, 1913), p. 14.

[2] For discussion of ornithology, see Thomas E. Lones, *Aristotle's Researches in Natural Science* (London, 1912), pp. 241 ff.

[3] According to D'Arcy W. Thompson (*Glossary of Greek Birds,* 2d ed., London, Oxford University Press, 1936, p. 86), much eagle lore was based on the habits of the vulture, especially the griffon vulture.

note the consistent evidence of interdependence of poets and scientists from the beginning. Aristotle quoted Homer and Hesiod on occasion, though Vergil marks the true beginning of the interdependence. In the *Georgics,* which contains most of his references to birds, it appears that Vergil drew not only from the Greek poets—Homer, Hesiod, Theocritus, and Aratus—but from Aristotle's *History of Animals.* But he is not to be denied firsthand observation. Warde Fowler remarks, "There is hardly to be found, in the whole of Virgil's poems, a single allusion to the habits of birds or any other animals which is untrue to fact as we know it from Italian naturalists."[4] After Vergil, both poetry and prose were soon to abandon all attempt to regard birds as living creatures.

It may be useful to illustrate Vergil's characteristic manner. Much of the *Georgics* is devoted to birds as weather signs. Homer had noted cranes fleeing from the winter cold and rain. So in Vergil, when the heron flies high, for example, a storm is imminent. "It quits its home in the marsh and soars aloft above the clouds."[5] Here, it happens, the poet was more intent upon Lucan than upon nature; but this idea about herons was adopted by the later encyclopedists, Isidore and Bartholomew, for example, and echoed verbatim through the centuries. The nightingale provides further illustration. When the poet wrote of this bird, rejecting the ubiquitous legend of Philomela, he provided a rational though equally false explanation of what appeared

[4] Warde Fowler, *A Year with the Birds* (6th ed., London, 1914), p. 215.

[5] *Virgil,* tr. Rushton Fairclough (2 vols., Cambridge, Loeb Classical Library, 1937), I, p. 107. *Geor.* i, 363–64: "Notasque paludes deserit atque altam supra volat ardea nubem."

to him as the sadness of its song: "Even as the nightingale, mourning beneath the poplar's shade, bewails the loss of her brood, that a churlish plowman hath espied and torn unfledged from the nest: but she weeps all night long, and, perched on a spray, renews her piteous strain, filling the region round with sad laments."[6]

But, paradoxically, even Plato in this regard proved a better naturalist: "No bird sings when it is cold or hungry, or is afflicted with any other pain, not even the nightingale, or swallow, or the hoopoes, which they say sing lamenting through grief."[7] In classical verse the nightingale has played varied roles, roles which, it will appear, typify the interpretation in English poetry of birds generally.[8]

For present purposes the long story of natural history in the first centuries of the Christian era must be abridged. The greatest—that is, the most prolix as well as most influential—of the Roman compilers is Pliny (first century); lesser figures are Aelian and Solinus (third century), Claudian (fourth century), and Cassiodorus (sixth century). True encyclopedists—their method philological rather than scientific—they labored to assemble all extant information from written and oral sources. The symbolic approach is evident even in Pliny, who regarded all animals as instruments for man's service—ethical, utilitarian, and aesthetic.

[6] *Ibid.*, p. 233; *Geor.* iv, 511–15: "Qualis populea maerens philomela sub umbra amissos queritu fetus, quos durus arator observans nido implumis detraxit; at illa flet noctem, ramoque sedens miserabile carmen integrat, et maestis late loca quaestibus implet."

[7] *Five Dialogues of Plato,* Henry Cary, tr. *Phaedo,* 85 (Everyman edition), p. 161.

[8] See Albert R. Chandler, "The Nightingale in Greek and Latin Poetry," *Classical Journal,* XXX (1934), pp. 78–84. For its place in English poetry, see pp. 27 ff., 46, 59, 87.

For the Christian Church Neo-Platonism was at work not only to confirm this attitude but wholly to establish earth's creatures as God's beneficent instruments in raising man's thoughts to Him. "The letter killeth, but the spirit giveth life"; the material exists only for the sake of the spiritual. Learning, or philology, therefore, is the deriving of the higher meaning from earth's lowly life. Apparent as early as Augustine's *City of God,* this attitude was universal by the seventh century. The case is well stated by Charles E. Raven:

> Aristotle seems merely the name of a remote and legendary sage, just as Virgil is evidently the mythical wizard and necromancer. And this is characteristic; for in science as in philosophy and religion, the achievements of Greek and Classical Roman civilisation had by this time been transmuted into a traditional lore in which a recognisable nucleus of original authority could scarcely be disinterred from the mass of glosses, accretions, syncretisms, and moralising which pious imagination and fear had imposed upon it. The same influences which produced the legends of the saints produced also these tales of eagles and wrens, of foxes and bears and lions.[9]

This outlook, then, gave rise to a learned tradition in which the visible phenomena in nature were of no account; in fact, to the visible world the mass of traditional data bore little or no resemblance. But outside this learned circle, on a lower level, men still cherished a lively interest in the life of animals around them. Such natural interest is evident even in the writings of those who shared the attitude of the learned; but it is with this innate curiosity that

[9] Charles E. Raven, *English Naturalists from Neckam to Ray* (London, Cambridge University Press, 1947), p. 6.

the beginnings of science may be identified. The parallel course of the two traditions may now be traced in brief detail.

For the Church Fathers the divine work of the first six days became the all-important theme of homilies which stood as supreme authority for future ages. The importance of Basil the Great, supreme among the hexaemeral writers, is touched upon in the later chapter on Milton, whose reverence for the tradition, as for Basil himself, is intimately reflected in both his prose and his poetic account of creation.

In the light of modern times it is customary to smile at the marvels in that great mine of morality, the *Physiologus*. But in its proper light this guide to God's ways with men is a monument of reverent cogitation.

Theological writers were not in the least prepared to question the worth of the marvelous description of creatures that were current in the schools on the faith of authorities vaguely known as "the history of animals," "the naturalists," and "the naturalist" in the singular number (Φυσιλόγος). So they took their notions of strange beasts and other marvels of the visible world on trust, and did their best to make them available for religious instruction.[10]

Furthermore, as Bush remarks, "If much of the traditional lore of nature that was considered true was not true, the fact of untruth had small bearing on the validity of the symbol."[11] Arising in the fourth century, influencing later writers as it was influenced by earlier, the *Physiologus* was a boon to the homilist, to the creator of architectural fig-

[10] "Physiologus," *Encyclopaedia Britannica* (11th ed.). Quoted by permission.

[11] Douglas Bush, *Science and English Poetry* (New York, 1950), p. 12.

ures, and to the author of heraldic treatise. A typical *Physiologus,* or "bestiary," as its adaptations are called, is that compiled in the eleventh century by Bishop Theobald of Monte Cassino. Of the Eagle:

Often so curved is the beak of the bird when he seizes his
 victim
Scarce is he able to tear pieces from some of his prey;
Striking the same on a rock, and gnawing the food as he
 tears it,
Rubs he the curve of his beak thus on a rock gets his food. . . .
Prayers of his mouth are heard, if asked of the Father for
 Christ's sake,
Christ is indeed the Rock, so the Apostle has said.

The explanation follows:

So also the sinner, by striking on the Rock, which is Christ, with humble prayers and entreaties for forgiveness, in confessing his sins, gets rid of this distortion of his mouth, that is sin, so that after this he is able to take food, that is the grace of God. Whence the author shows how Christ is signified by the rock. The Apostle saying: "The Rock indeed was Christ."

Of a different bird:

Doves like the turtle vainly love never,
Mated to one love, clings to him ever, . . .
Thus the soul stands fast faithful forever, . . .
Christ is its true Spouse also its dear Lord.

So any faithful soul, once linked to its Spouse, namely Christ in baptism, always ought to remain at His side in well-doing day and night, so that from Christ it should never be separated by sinning mortally.[12]

[12] *Physiologus: A Metrical Bestiary of Twelve Chapters by Bishop*

As its origins suggest both Aesop's fables and Christ's parables, so this symbolic application is taken over by the encyclopedias of knowledge. Immensely significant in its influence upon poetry, this genre now deserves attention.

Of the early encyclopedists the greatest name is Isidore of Seville (seventh century). The title of his masterpiece suggests its method: *Etymologiarum libri XX.*[13] As Ernest Brehaut remarks: "The road to knowledge was by way of words, and further, they were to be elucidated by reference to their origin rather than to the things they stood for."[14] "Birds are called *aves* because they have no definite paths, but wander through all pathless ('avia') ways. . . . It is certain that many names of birds are formed from the sound of the voice, such as *grus, corvus, cygnus, pavo;* . . . indeed the variety of their voices has taught men what they should be named."[15] From word derivation, Isidore, the objective scholar, turned to Aristotle, Cicero, Suetonius, Pliny, and Solinus, to Moses, Jerome, Ambrose, Paul, Origen, and Augustine, as well as to Vergil, Ovid, and Martial for information which, despite Brehaut's strictures,[16] he presented

---

Theobald, tr. Alan W. Rendell (London, 1928), pp. 9–10, 41–43. Theobald was Abbot at Monte Cassino, 1022–35. The present work was first printed in Cologne in 1492.

13 Migne, *Patrologiae Latinae,* LXXXII. Birds occupy Bk. 12, Chap. 7, pp. 459–70.

14 Ernest Brehaut, "An Encyclopaedist of the Dark Ages: Isidore of Seville," *Columbia University Studies in History, Economics, and Public Law,* XLVIII (1912), p. 33.

15 "*Aves* dictae, eo quod vias certas non habeant, sed per *avia* quaeque discurrant. . . . Avium nomina multa a sono vocis constat esse composita, ut grus, corvus, cygnus, pavo, . . . varietas enim vocis eorum docuit homines quid nominarentur." (Migne, *op. cit.,* p. 459.)

16 For example: "Their minds, not being irritated or roused by any perception of inconsistency, rest happy in the conviction that all is explained, and remain oblivious of that sense of mystery which forms the background of modern scientific thought." (Brehaut, *op. cit.,* p. 49.)

in orderly manner without moralizing. And, it should be remembered, the encyclopedist does not necessarily subscribe to all matter fit for inclusion. As has been more fairly observed, "The 'Libri Etymologiarum' supplied the following centuries not only with a concise and fairly accurate précis of education but included as well all contemporary knowledge."[17] Isidore's nature lore echoes loudly through the centuries ahead. To prevent sleep, sentry cranes hold stones in their claws (see Figure 9). Storks (*ciconiae* "as if *cicaniae,* which, it is established, is more a noise of the bill than a note because they make it by clattering the bill"[18]) are the spring harbingers, serpents' enemies; they fly across seas, arriving in Asia in close formation. Ostriches neglect to incubate their eggs, which, cast at random, are hatched in the warmth of the dust. The owl (*ulula*) is named from its plaint and groan. In winter, the solitary turtle, having lost its feathers, is destined to hibernate in hollow tree trunks. The rock dove (*Columba*) bills lasciviously; the chaste wood dove (*palumbes*) never takes a second mate. Cuckoos arrive in spring perched on the backs of kites, for they would otherwise fail in their long flight. Isidore classed bats with birds but observed carefully their distinction in anatomy, flight, and note.

Such factual information amassed from every available source typifies this, the first thorough compilation; and for a millennium it was quoted and respected by every writer on natural history. According to Brehaut, complete editions were issued in Paris in 1580, in Madrid in 1599, and in

[17] Curt Bühler, "The Sources of the Court of Sapience," *Beitrage zur Englischen Philologie,* XXIII (Leipzig, 1932), p. 64.

[18] "Quasi çicaniae, quem sonum oris potius esse (constat) quam vocis, quia eum quatiente rostro faciunt." (Migne, *op. cit.,* p. 462.)

Folger Shakespeare Library

1. The first illustration of birds in a book printed in England. (From *Bartholomeus de proprietatibus rerum,* tr. Trevisa, printed by Wynken de Worde, 1495.)

Paris in 1600. Between 1477 and 1577 ten editions have been counted. Earlier, its influence was also pervasive in such encyclopedias as that of Bartholomew, where every page bears the impress of Isidore's authority.

For the poetic tradition in England, the *De proprietati-*

bus rerum by Bartholomeus Anglicus was to prove an important guide in both creed and content. The earliest known manuscript of the work, now in the Bodleian, was written in 1296. According to Se Boyar,[19] over one hundred copies of the manuscript Latin text are extant in European libraries. In 1286 at the University of Paris the book was listed as one to be lent to students, and during the next two centuries it was translated into six European languages. Forty-six printed editions have been identified. This great work was translated into English in 1397 by John de Trevisa, the English version being printed in 1495 by Wynkyn de Worde, in 1535 by Thomas Berthelet, and in 1582 edited by Stephen Batman.[20] The last, entitled *Batman uppon Bartholome . . .*, endeavored to bring the ancient lore up to date; on birds Batman often cited Gesner, whose work will be mentioned later. Earlier, in 1567, Trevisa's version was abridged by Maplet and issued as *The Greene Forest* without acknowledgment. Such was the enormous popularity of the work.

Se Boyar believes that Bartholomew knew Aristotle in translations from the Arabians, who also supplied commentary. Raven, who has given attention to Bartholomew's sources, mentions "a small nucleus of material drawn from Michael Scot's Aristotle and having some remote resemblance to fact" (p. 14). The translation by Scot had been

[19] Gerald E. Se Boyar, "Bartholomeus Anglicus and His Encyclopaedia," *Journal of English and Germanic Philology,* XIX (1920), pp. 168–89, especially pp. 183–88.

[20] An important descendant of Bartholomew's work is the fifteenth-century [*H*]*ortus Sanitatis,* of which many versions were issued. The division on birds appears first in the "larger *Hortus*" of 1491. See Arnold Klebs, "Incunabula Lists: Herbals," *Papers of the Bibliographical Society of America,* XII (1918), pp. 41–57.

made by order of the Emperor Frederick II (1194–1250), whose huge treatise on falconry also includes much first-hand information on various other birds. According to Wood, Aristotle was almost the sole authority recognized by Frederick, who even so did not hesitate to contradict the Greek.[21] This approach sorely contrasts with that of Bartholomew, with whom Isidore stood as chief authority, with Pliny and the hexaemeral writers next in prominence. Except perhaps for the protracted discussion of hawks in Chapter 2, perhaps indebted to Frederick, the work bears no evidence that author or translator possessed any interest in observing birds or in listening to reports of other men who had done so.

In his Preface, Bartholomew states his philosophy of nature:

> As a man is ledde by the hande, so by these formes visible, our wit may be ledde to the consideration of the greatnes or magnitude of the most excellent beauteous claretie, divine and invisible. Also, the blessed Apostle Paule in his Epistle, reciteth this, saieng: that by these things visibles, which are made and be visible, man may see and know by his inwarde sight intellectual, the divine, celestiall, and godlye things, which are invissibles to this our naturale sight.

Little wonder that in exploring Spenser's similes from nature one finds their origins in Bartholomew, who so explicitly laid his world upon Platonic foundations. "The

[21] *The Art of Falconry: Being the de arte venandi cum avibus of Frederick II of Hohenstaufan,* tr. and ed. Casey A. Wood and F. Marjorie Fyfe (Stanford, Calif., Stanford University Press, 1943), p. xxxix. Wood mentions a single Latin edition, in 1596. The moralistic tradition was too firmly entrenched to admit Frederick, who as student of birds stands alone and without perceptible influence except perhaps in the field of falconry.

allegorical instinct," remarks Bush, "is closely related to the poetic instinct, since a poet works through metaphor and symbol" (p. 12). Signal illustration of this truth is disclosed by comparing the creed of Bartholomew, quoted above, with the conception of the poet's function in the words of Sir Philip Sidney. The poet, declares Sidney:

> making things either better then nature bringeth foorth, or, quite a new, formes such as never were in nature . . . goeth hand in hand with nature, not enclosed within the narrow warrant of her gifts but freely raunging within the Zodiack of his owne wit. Nature never set foorth the earth in so rich Tapistry as diverse Poets have done, neither with so pleasaunt rivers, fruitfull trees, sweete smelling flowers, nor whatsoever els may make the too much loved earth more lovely: her world is brasen, the Poets only deliver a golden. . . . The heavenly maker of that maker . . . set him beyond and over all the workes of that second nature; which in nothing he sheweth so much as in Poetry; when with the force of a divine breath, he bringeth things foorth far surpassing her doings, with no small arguments to the incredulous of that first accursed fall of *Adam,* since our erected wit maketh us to know what perfection is, and yet our infected wil keepeth us from reaching unto it. But these arguments will by few be understood, and by fewer granted. . . . The finall end is, to lead and draw us to as high a perfection, as our degenerate soules made worse by their clay-lodgings, can be capable of.[22]

This is eloquent testimony of the completeness with which the Aristotelian approach to nature had been obscured through Platonic influence. So far as nature is con-

[22] *The Defence of Poesie,* ed. Albert Feuillerat (London, Cambridge University Press, 1923), pp. 8 ff.

cerned, Sidney's was still the world of the *Physiologus* and Bartholomew. Later consideration of Spenser includes frequent analogues from Bartholomew, who need not, then, be further quoted here.

So much for the encyclopedic tradition, which was moralistic, learned, removed from the actual world. It now remains to call attention to another tradition, unlearned and spontaneous, and as important to the growth of science as the learned tradition was to poetry. Raven observes (p. 26): "This deep-seated native delight in the woods and valleys, the plants and the birds of the country, an aesthetic, almost a religious, rather than an intellectual experience, may well be regarded, more truly than the fables and moralizings of Bartholomew and his fellow-scholars, as the sources of our scientific achievements." Its roots in the English love of gardens and of hunting, this native tradition is "preserved more truly in the quaint dialect names of flowers and birds than in the legends of the clerks." For centuries the two traditions existed side by side. Moreover, just as poets reflect both ways of thought, so in earlier times the two approaches to nature are paradoxically evident in works on natural history. This important phenomenon may be exemplified in the work of two twelfth-century monks, Alexander Neckam and Giraldus de Barri, or Giraldus Cambrensis.

Neckam compiled the *De naturis rerum libri duo*[23] as a manual of scientific knowledge; Chapter 23 of the first book treats of birds, a total of forty. Primarily the author aimed to repeat the best scientific data extant—from Aris-

[23] With *De laudibus divinae sapientiae*, ed. Thomas Wright (London, 1863).

totle, Pliny, Solinus, and Cassiodorus; from Ovid, Claudian, and Martial; and from Hildebertus, or Bishop Hildebert, contemporary author of a *Physiologus.* Isidore's etymologies and moralizings, original and otherwise, lend their full weight: *alauda* (lark) derives from *laus,* "praise," as the bird rises from earth to greet the sun; "the dove has a kind of moan instead of a song, setting forth the type of the blessed church or even some faithful soul. For in this vale of tears we ought to moan, so that we may come to the place of rejoicing." Thus "nature in truth instructs us in many things." By purging "itself with its bill, the stork [usually it is the ibis] taught man the use of the clyster." In contradiction to the usual observation of this bird's migratory habits, Neckam states: "In winter also it lies hid in waters, but in the springtime, leaving the realms of the Naiads, glad harbinger of the more clement air, it lives in the open. Thus, thus, blessed men, hourly rendering to God what is His, rejoice in the winter of this life under a lowly habit, awaiting the delights of summer to come."[24] This analogy, perhaps also original, is wholly in the manner of the *Physiologus.* But in Cassiodorus, Neckam finds the stork the prime example of piety, loyalty, and gratitude (pp. 112–13). If it discovers unfaithfulness in its mate, the stork summons its fellows, and together they tear the criminal to pieces; and in their old age the parents are

24 "Columba siquidem gemitum habet pro cantu, sanctae ecclesiae vel etiam cuius cunque fidelis animae typum gerens. In hac namque valle lacrimarum gemere debemus, ut ad locum exultationis veniamus." Thus "Natura vero nos in multis informat. . . . In hieme huius autem latet in aquis, sed verno tempore Naiadum regna linquens, sub divo degit elementioris aurae laeta salutatrix. Sic et viri sancti singulis horis Deo quod suum est persolventes, in hieme huius vitae latitant sub humili habitu, aestatis futurae delicias expectantes." (*Ibid.,* pp. 106, 112.)

fed by their young (see Chapter II, "Chaucer," page 39).[25] Sin thus finds its reward. A characteristic turn is given the story of how the wren hides in the eagle's plumage and, mounting its back after an upward flight, proclaims itself king (*regulus*) of birds: "This fable comes home to those who, entering into the labors of others, presume to transfer to themselves the glory due others."[26]

But Neckam gives life to this otherwise conventional treatise by means of anecdotes from hearsay or actual experience. His real delight in storytelling resulted in vivid pictures of medieval life, showing, as his editor remarks, "how ready people apparently of all classes were to observe and note the peculiarities of animated nature, and especially how fond they were of tamed and domestic animals" (pp. 20–21). On one occasion an eagle is killed by a hawk in self-defense, in full view of the applauding courtiers, who are promptly scolded by their king for praising the use of force by vassals. In the same vein Neckam relates that in winter the hawk seizes a duck or partridge and holds it under its belly all night to profit from its warmth but at dawn, however hungry, releases its benefactor. This act, writes Neckam, typifies the ideal feudal baron. An eagle has killed one of a pair of falcons. Using a hole in a bridge, the survivor traps and kills its enemy.

[25] "Aelian writeth of a storke, which bred on the house of one who had a very beautiful wife, which in her husband's absence used to commit adultery with one of her base servants: which the storke observing, in gratitude to him who freely gave him house-roome, flying in the villaines face, strucke out both his eyes." (John Guillim, *A Display of Heraldrie,* Sec. 3, Chap. 19.) See Chapter IV, "Milton," p. 95, n. 12.

[26] "Haac relatio fabulosa illos tangit qui aliarum labores intrantes, gloriam aliis debitam in se praesumunt transferre." (Neckam, *op. cit.,* p. 123.)

This episode occurred in the vicinity of Rouen, whose citizens witnessed the act. True or not, in thus localizing natural phenomena, Neckam anticipated an important phase of scientific method.

Overshadowed as it was by the tradition of the encyclopedia, Neckam's work was yet to prove important for Chaucer. Even before, its influence was pervasive in the uniquely realistic poem *The Owl and the Nightingale,* to be discussed later. Thus Chaucer's realistic vein was not without notable precedent in verse.

If Neckam dimly anticipated scientific method, his contemporary Giraldus Cambrensis, drawing at times from the *De naturis rerum,* proved the better naturalist. An observant traveler, Giraldus included a remarkably accurate account of birds in his *Topography of Ireland* (1188).[27] For example, he adopted Neckam's fanciful account of the submersion of storks in winter, but followed with a description of the hibernation of other birds (still a question) and of dormice: "During this period they are neither living nor dead, but vegetating without the breath of life being extinct, they appear wrapt in a long trance, and, remaining without the nourishment by which animal life is wont to be sustained, are yet supported by some kind and secret process of nature, until, roused from their sleep, they come back with the zephyrs and the first swallow" (p. 40).

Moreover, Giraldus skilfully distinguished a number of birds with attention to their appearance, food, and habits: kingfisher, crow, shrike, and duck. The account of the hatching of barnacle geese from ships' timber was respect-

[27] *Historical Works of Giraldus Cambrensis,* tr. Sir Richard C. Hoare, rev. and ed. Thomas Wright (London, 1863), pp. 39–40.

Folger Shakespeare Library

2. Hibernating swallows drawn with fish from water. (From Olaus Magnus, *Historia de gentibus septentrionalibus* . . . , Rome, 1555, p. 673.)

fully quoted by William Turner (1544); the description of the osprey—one foot webbed, the other clawed—was disputed by John Caius (1570)—evidence that Giraldus was read with interest by later scientists. Other works, too, are important in this connection. The *Itinerary through Wales* (1191) contains an observant note on the difference between green woodpecker and golden oriole. Even in his *Anglia Sacra,* twice, as Raven notes (p. 24), Giraldus found occasion to point out differences between the two swans, wild and tame, a distinction unrecognized by scientists until the seventeenth century (see Chapter V, "Drayton," pages 122–23). Yet this remarkable observer abundantly shared the old, learned outlook, for he rarely lost opportunity to draw a moral and to repeat the timeworn symbolism. But as his editor, James F. Dimock, remarks (V, p. lxxi), "He was also an acute observer, and had the boldness to put his own observations by the side of the received traditions." Much drawn from Neckam, these observations need no further illustration. The important point is that the discovery of truths by observation was fully evident during the Middle Ages even when, pressed by church and state, men learned, accepted, and lived by the supposed truths of a marvelous world of legend and symbol.

In the centuries following Neckam and Giraldus, not unnaturally the learned world of the encyclopedia, perpetuating the old, continued to eclipse the unrecognized world of observation. Yet such a work as Caxton's *Mirrour of the World* (1489) gave promise of the slow change. This book, the first printed in England with descriptions of birds,[28] repeats much of the old lore, yet shows interest in relating birds to their native lands. Omitting all moralizing, Caxton submitted his translation so that a man "may the better avaylle in knowleche alle the dayes of his lyf" (p. 7). When, a little more than a half-century later, William Turner undertook to identify the birds of Aristotle and Pliny, his purposes were not significantly different from those of Caxton.

Turner fully realized the approach to nature which be-

[28] Oliver H. Prior (ed.), *Early English Text Society,* ex. ser. CX (1913). This translation from the French *Image du Monde,* by Gossouin, was first issued in 1480–81, was reprinted by Caxton in 1489 and by Lawrence Andrew in 1527. As the first such in England, it is listed by Ramon Irwin, *British Bird Books: An Index to British Ornithology, 1481–1948* (London, 1951).

fore had been casual but persistent. "The change which shattered the old world picture," observes Raven (p. 22), "was not the discovery of the world of nature, but the recovery of the Greek and Latin classics." Actually, the study of Aristotle and Pliny led Turner to observation as a necessary means of identifying their birds. It will be profitable now to refer briefly to Turner's purposes in his great work on birds and to mention some directions of accomplishment.

The originality of Turner's work on birds is not suggested by its title: *Avium praecipuarum apud Plinium et Aristotelem mentio est, brevis et succincta historia* (Cologne, 1544).[29] Yet much of the work involved the separating of the Greek generic names into species and supplying local English names.[30] From his own observations he often corrected or amended the Greek descriptions. Like his predecessors, he freely cited the poets to his purpose, yet he was the first to note their limitations. Rejecting an identification in Aristophanes of two species of gulls as one, Turner adopted Aristotle's distinction. For after all, he stated, poets "observe more negligently than philosophers the peculiar properties of things and their diversities" (pp. 74–75). The tone of the entire treatise is one of

[29] *Turner on Birds,* ed., with introduction, translation, and notes, A. H. Evans (Cambridge, 1903). An appendix presents the short treatise of John Caius, *De rariorum animalium* (1570), in translation, to be referred to in connection with Drayton. The following discussion has been condensed from Thomas P. Harrison, "William Turner, Naturalist and Priest," *University of Texas Studies in English,* XXXIII (1954), pp. 1–12.

[30] "If we remove from his 130 recognizable birds those which are domestic or were not seen in Britain, we are left with 105 species . . . of which no less than thirty-seven have appeared as British birds in no previous document, manuscript or printed, that I have seen or heard of." (James Fisher, *A History of Birds,* Boston, 1954, p. 20.)

careful conjecture, for which the author apologized in an introductory address to the reader. Yet, he added, it is better, "on a subject that is difficult and not yet sufficiently explored, to tread doubtingly and modestly by conjecture and so to enquire, than to pronounce rashly and immodestly on things undetermined" (p. 185). "Inquirere quam pronunciare": these words mark the beginning of the new spirit of inquiry.

On the subject of migration, for example, even today the greatest of bird mysteries, Turner was consistently guarded; on Aristotle's opinions he declined comment, for he lacked evidence to the contrary. Unlike his Swedish contemporary, Olaus Magnus (see Figure 2), Turner was silent on the classical theory of hibernation.[31] But with Aristotle's belief in the transmutation of one species into another Turner took issue, for he was aware of the arrival of certain birds at the time that others departed. On the robin-redstart change, Turner objected that Aristotle, "relying on the tales of fowlers more than on his own experience, has wandered greatly from the path of truth" (p. 155); and he presented detailed evidence to support his denial of this ancient and unnatural belief.[32]

But Turner the scientist was also priest and fervid reformer driven from England by Antichrist. In his savage

[31] For Charles Morton's theory of migration to the moon (1686), see Thomas P. Harrison, "Birds in the Moon," *Isis,* XLV (1954), pp. 323–30.

[32] Aristotle's delusion probably arose from the fact that "the Redbreast appears in Greece in winter after most of the Redstarts have gone away southward." (Warde Fowler, *Summer Studies of Birds and Books,* London, 1895, p. 183.) On Turner's description of the nests of robins, see David Lack, *The Life of the Robin* (London, 1953), pp. 87–89. On transmutation he remarks (p. 114) that "the problem was easier for Turner since both species nested where he lived," i.e., in Northumberland.

church tracts it is interesting to note the prominent role of birds as the author permitted his natural history to return to the Middle Ages. Ten years after the scientific treatise, Turner, in attacking Bishop Stephen Gardiner, who had changed from Anglican fox into Catholic wolf, supported his contention with several of Aristotle's examples of transmutation (*The Hunting of the Romish Wolf,* 1554). In the Latin scientific treatise, Turner was intent upon the letter; in his office as priest warning his countrymen against false prophets, he was concerned only with the spirit, and to it the world of nature gives life. Turner deeply believed that the animal world, including birds, was divinely provided to set forth examples for humanity. To this extent, then, the religious controversialist looked backward rather than forward, and Turner's hybrid genius was consistent with that of earlier writers who have been mentioned. The medieval habit of using examples from nature for satirical ends was perpetuated by Milton; Turner the scientist occasionally reappeared in Spenser; and both satirical and scientific aspects are exemplified in Drayton.

Theoretically the interpretations of nature in terms of moralistic symbol based upon untried legend, on the one hand, and in terms of observed fact, on the other, appear entirely distinct. The writings of early naturalists consistently prove the contrary, and it is possible only to note which approach is the more pervasive. The tradition of the encyclopedia was guided by a philosophy which was translated into poetic terms by Sidney and Spenser. Yet Bartholomew was less intent upon morality than was Neckam. Moreover, one is reminded, Bartholomew's emphasis upon falconry anticipated the series of such practical disserta-

He beareth *Azure*, a *Bend Argent*, *Cottized Or*, betweene ſix *Martlets* of the ſame. This *Coat-armour* pertaineth to the ancient Familie of *de Labere*, whereof *Richard de Labere* of *Sowtham* in the *County* of *Gloceſter Eſquire*, is lineally deſcended. The *Martlet* or *Martinet* (ſaith *Bekenhawb*) hath legges ſo exceeding ſhort, that they can by no meanes goe: and thereupon it ſeemeth the *Grecians* doe call them *Apodes*, *quaſi ſine pedibus*, not becauſe they doe *want feet*, but becauſe they haue not ſuch vſe of their *feet* as other *birds* haue.

He beareth *Argent*, a *Heron volant* in *Feſſe Azure*, *membred Or*, betweene three *Eſcallops Sable*, by the name of *Herondon*. Heere alſo you ſee one geſture of a *Fowle volant*, in the carriage of his legges, which was not before exemplied. *Pliny* ſaith, that all *Fowles* that ſtalke with *long ſhankes*, as they flie they doe ſtretch out their *legges* in length to their *tailes*; but ſuch as are ſhort legged, doe draw them vp to the midſt of their bellies.

Folger Shakespeare Library

3. Martins (*above*) and heron (*below*). (From John Guillim, *A Display of Heraldrie,* 1611, pp. 163, 172.)

tions as Dame Berners' *Boke of St. Alban's* (1496) and, in Spenser's time, Turberville's *Booke of Faulconrie* (1575). Turner's monumental treatise on birds was followed, eleven years later, by his friend Gesner's *De avium natura* (Zurich, 1555) and by Belon's *Histoire de la Nature des Oiseaux* (Paris, 1555), both strictly scientific accomplishments. Yet on the popular level the world of the encyclopedia dominated the sixteenth century.

As this tradition gradually waned, the symbolic approach to nature continued to survive in books of emblems and of heraldry. Alciati and his successors, such as Geoffrey Whitney (*Choice of Emblemes,* 1586), survive in Spenser. Less narrowly circumscribed than the emblem book, the heraldic treatise reflects the advances in natural knowledge which are superimposed upon the basic traditional interpretations. Examples are Gerard Legh's *Accedence of Armorie* (1562) and John Guillim's *Display of Heraldrie* (1610) (see Figure 3). The latter especially went afield to present a full dissertation on birds (Sec. 2, Chaps. 19–21), even occasionally quoting Belon (p. 217). Both these books were several times reprinted in the sixteenth and seventeenth centuries. Thus the two genres, essentially symbolic in aim, took their place alongside a new science shorn of moralizing and based upon observation. Their vogue helps to explain the persistence of ancient symbol in the bird lore of poetry, to which it is now appropriate to turn.

Poetry

The preceding account has had to do with the intellectual background out of which gradually arose the new science of observation. It will be profitable now to note briefly the manner in which birds were adapted to become literary convention.

Although the poetry of Chaucer retains vestiges of moralizing from nature, he learned quickly to transmute bird symbolism to the secular level. In this process may be discerned the influence of three poetic devices in which birds are involved: the debate, the mass, and the catalogue. All are closely knit with the court of love. Since their origin and diffusion have been fully explored by Neilson[33] and others, they demand attention here only as background for Chaucer's *The Parlement of Foules,* for Milton's nightingale sonnet, and for Drayton's *The Owle.*

The bird debate is most conspicuously represented in *The Owl and the Nightingale,* written 1189–1217 by Nicholas or John of Guildford.[34] Following the procedure of a thirteenth-century lawsuit, this poem presents the nightingale as plaintiff in behalf of the new love poetry as against the owl, who stands for religious, didactic verse. Eros triumphs, as might be expected of a poet obviously announcing the new order. The greater triumph, however, lies in the poet's art of conducting the debate wholly on the bird level.

This point deserves elaboration. As Atkins points out, Neckam is the poet's chief source. Even the introduction of two fables—concerning owl and falcon, and cat and fox—is in the manner of the poet's contemporary, as are more directly various points descriptive of the birds and their habits. The nightingale dominates the poem. From *De naturis rerum* Guildford noted the bird's absence from Scotland and Ireland, "loca multo frigori obnoxia," as Neckam observed, and he gracefully introduced its migrating habits. The owl chants woefully in winter. "But I all happiness with me bring," returns the nightingale; "every creature is glad because of me. . . . Blossoms burst forth and unfold themselves on the trees and in the meadows. The lily with her lovely hue welcomes me. . . . Yet never is my song too

[33] William A. Neilson, *The Origins and Sources of the Court of Love* (Boston, 1899).

[34] *The Owl and the Nightingale,* tr. and ed. J. W. H. Atkins (London, Cambridge University Press, 1922).

long. . . . When the thoughts of men are on harvest sheaves, and autumn brown doth stain the leaves, then I go home and take my leave, . . . taking with me love and thanks for my presence and my pains" (Atkins, p. 159). Excepting of course the Ovidian motif, which for the Renaissance was to become supreme, the traditional roles of the nightingale are present. As herald of spring (433 ff.), this is the nightingale of Pliny and Chaucer, where it "clepeth forth the leves newe." The bird is also the glad minstrel of divine praises (735 ff., 1036), and of love (1339 ff.).

Throughout *The Owl and the Nightingale* the poet's allegory does no violence to the actual natures of these avian contenders. In fact, their true appearance and their ways of life are inseparable from the matter of debate. In these respects the poem is unique, for in turning to the next great example of bird debate, one finds no such happy combination of realism and dialectic.

The Cuckoo and the Nightingale, long ascribed to Chaucer but, as Skeat finds,[35] written by Clanvowe (ca. 1392), shares both the debate motif and the court of love tradition, in which the divine nightingale is ever preferred to the cuckoo. Half asleep, the poet hears "that sory bird, the lewde cukkow" as it inveighs against Love and his servants. The indignant nightingale replies at length (149 ff.):

For in this worlde is noon so good servyse
To every wight that gentil is of kinde;
For there-of, trewly, cometh al goodnesse
Al honour, and eke al gentilnesse. . . .

[35] W. W. Skeat (ed.), *Chaucerian and Other Pieces: A Supplement to the Poems of Chaucer* (London, Oxford University Press, 1897), pp. 347 ff.

The poet soon takes sides and drives the cuckoo away with a stone, whereupon the nightingale promises that next May the poet will hear her before the cuckoo. Skeat first noted (p. lxi) that this poem was the basis for Milton's well-known sonnet, to be considered later.

Ultimately, of course, the cuckoo's parasitic habits were responsible for the ill repute it suffered in literary tradition. The evil nature of this bird as it appears in poems by Clanvowe, Chaucer, and Milton (but not by Spenser), may possibly be traced to its role in *La Messe des Oisiaus,* by Jean de Condé (ca. 1275–1340), the most elaborate example of the religious service sung by birds in honor of Venus. Twice in the course of the singing, which the nightingale shares prominently, the cuckoo interrupts and is pursued.[36]

The desire to distinguish the roles of birds was explicitly represented in staging a debate, with the lugubrious, owl-like religious songs contrasted with the light happiness of the nightingale lays, the disrupting profanity of the cuckoo against the divine theme of the nightingale.[37] The medieval *débat* then gave way to the antiphonal chorus of the assembled birds, and poems based upon this motif are legion.

[36] In the nursery rhyme "Cock Robin's Marriage to Jenny Wren" (1806), written "with the idea of making it a forerunner of the already well-established rhyme 'The death and burial of Cock Robin,' " the cuckoo interrupts the ceremony. The sparrow shoots at the intruder, but

"The cuckoo he missed and Cock Robin he killed."

The burial poem is believed to have originated in the fourteenth century. See Iona Opie and Peter Opie, *The Oxford Dictionary of Nursery Rhymes* (New York, Oxford University Press, 1951), pp. 129–33.

[37] For a full study of the changing role of the medieval nightingale, see J. M. Telfer, "The Evolution of a Medieval Theme," *Durham University Journal,* XLV (1952), pp. 25–34.

In such examples as *The Harmony of Birds*[38] and *Devotion of the Fowls*[39] the religious theme has replaced the secular, which was native to the court of love, with its association of birds with Venus. Thus the bird mass proper, conceived with religious fervor, is directly analogous to the moralistic encyclopedias.

As a reaction to the bird mass and as a brief-lived outgrowth the so-called "goliardic" verse arose in mockery. Venus of the court of love had disappeared, and birds gathered mournfully to burlesque the offices sung for the dead. In the first goliards sung by the wandering scholars, Bacchus replaced the Deity. Though even in Chaucer's time the word *goliardeys* had come to mean only "merry rogue," or "janglere," the sixteenth century witnessed a notable survival of the true goliard in John Skelton's *The Boke of Phyllyp Sparowe,* in which the poet's levity was directed not only at the church offices but also at the dubious lore of Pliny and the encyclopedists.

The third convention arising from bird assemblages, the catalogue, is involved in the bird mass. But in the mass, opportunity is afforded to adapt the traditional nature of the bird to its role in song. In its indiscriminate enumeration the mere catalogue allows no scope for the imagination: birds are merely listed with their traditional characteristics. The naming of the unclean birds in the Old Testament and the listing of trees in Homer provide precedent

[38] J. P. Collier (ed.), *Early English Poetry, Ballads, and Popular Literature of the Middle Ages* (London, Percy Society, 1842), VII. *The Harmony of Birds,* attributed to Skelton, was published in 1551.

[39] *A Selection from the Minor Poems of Dan John Lydgate,* ed. James O. Halliwell (London, Percy Society, 1840), pp. 78–80.

and background. Chaucer, it will be seen, adopted the catalogue from the example of Alanus de Insulis. Both debate and catalogue were to reappear in Drayton, who like Chaucer soon abandoned both for a more effective manner of introducing birds.

II : *Chaucer*

THE MEANINGLESS BIRD LISTS of the *Romaunt of the Rose* give little promise of Chaucer's later successes. "The statement of Langlois that more than five thousand verses of the *Roman de la Rose* are translated, imitated, or inspired by the *De Planctu Naturae* is excellent authority that this mysterious scholar of the Middle Ages, whose very identity is unascertained, was of those who beget kings in literature, though he himself were none," writes Douglas Moffat.[1] Thus the birds of the *Romaunt,* though not from Alanus (ca. 1128–1202), lead directly to those of the *Parlement of Foules,* which are. Comparison of the French text with Chaucer's rendering illustrates his method and his addition of new members. All the birds are named without distinction and hence remain mere names of singing birds which

By note made fair servyse.

The first passage comprises lines 657 to 665. The French original[2] names *estorniaus* (starlings), *roietiaus* (wrens), *torteroles* (turtledoves), *chardonnereaus* (goldfinches), *arondeles* (swallows), *aloes* (larks), *lardereles* (titmice), *calendres* (larks), and *mavis* (song thrush).

Chaucer makes some departures in the list, which includes alpes, finches, wodewales, turtles, laverokkes, chalaundres, thrustles, terins, and mavis. Here the poet omits starling, swallow, tit, and wren. Recognizing that not all birds may be found in one place, he writes of the first three that they sing

In thilke places as they habiten.

The "alpe," or bullfinch, Drayton calls "nope," a contraction of "an alp." Chaucer's "wodewale" is Turner's witwol (172–75), the golden oriole and a singing bird rather than the green woodpecker, which, sometimes termed *witwall,* is probably Chaucer's "popiniay," in a later passage.

[1] *Alain de Lille, The Complaint of Nature* (*Yale Studies in English,* XXXVI, New York, 1908), Preface.

[2] *The Romaunt of the Rose,* ed. W. W. Skeat (London, Oxford University Press, 1899).

Chaucer renders French *aloes* as "laverokkes" (larks, specifically skylarks); *calendres* he repeats as "chalaundres," possibly because the European calandra lark was unknown to him. The "terin" is the siskin, according to the *NED,* or another of the finches. "Thrustle" may be intended for the mistle thrush, though it was much later than Chaucer that the mavis (song thrush) was distinguished from this bird (see Index, page 150).

In the second French passage only four birds are named: *papegaus, rossignaus, calandres,* and *mesanges.* All but the last Chaucer renders easily: popiniay (green woodpecker), nightingale, and chalaundre (lark). He replaces the French *mésange* (titmouse) with wodewale, finch, lark, and archangel, possibly because he does not recognize the English equivalent. Chaucer's "archangel," a unique bird name, Skeat (p. 424) believes answers to *mésange* (tit). D'Arcy Thompson aptly suggests that Chaucer's word is a scribal corruption of *acaunthyl,* namely, *acanthyllis,* goldfinch or siskin; Kunstmann attempts to equate *archangel* and *wariangle,* Chaucer's name for the shrike (*Friar's Tale,* 1408).[3] The poet was concerned, he thinks, only with finding a rhyme word.

Chaucer indicates that his well-known list of birds in *The Parlement of Foules* is drawn directly after the embellished garment of Dame Nature in Alanus, "right as Aleyn, in the Pleynt of Kynde." Many theories have been advanced concerning particular identifications in Chaucer's

[3] D'Arcy W. Thompson, in *Notes and Queries,* CLXXV (November 5, 1938), p. 332; John G. Kunstmann, in *Modern Language Notes,* LV (1940), pp. 259–62. On Chaucer's "wariangel" (one of the shrikes) as a poisonous bird, see Thomas P. Harrison, in *Notes and Queries,* CXCIX (May, 1954), p. 189.

allegory, although, as Robinson remarks, "a personal application of the poem, though undeniably possible, still seems to be by no means necessary." But there is general agreement that Chaucer's four groups of birds "represent the different classes of society, the birds of prey standing for the nobles, the worm-fowl for the bourgeoisie, the seed-fowl for the agricultural class (or, according to some, for the clergy), and the water-fowl for the great merchants."[4] In this manner, ornithology subserves the poet's larger human intent. "That is to seyn," explains Chaucer (323 ff.):

the foules of ravyne
Weere hyest set, and thanne the foules smale;
That eten, as hem nature wolde enclyne,
As worm or thyng, of which I telle no tale;
And water-foul sat lowest in the dale,
But foul that lyveth by sed sat on the grene,
And that so fele that wonder was to sene.

Though the encyclopedists invariably describe birds alphabetically, they repeat with general fidelity Aristotle's able classification of birds according to their food, neglecting, however, that according to the anatomy of feet. Aristotle's six groups—those feeding on flesh, on grubs, on thistles, on insects, on fruit and herbage, and on fish and water plants (592b–593b)—are repeated as five by Vincent of Beauvais: "Some eat flesh, some grain, some either, some worms, some live on the shores of lakes and eat from them."[5] Thus Aristotle's careful attempt at classification is

[4] F. N. Robinson, *The Poetical Works of Chaucer* (Boston, 1933), pp. 901, 904.

[5] From *The Works of Chaucer,* ed. W. W. Skeat (London, Oxford University Press, 1894–97), I, p. 517:

transmitted through the Middle Ages with rare fidelity, all the more remarkable in view of the overwhelming regard for moral allegory. Chaucer affords this glimpse of the Greek scientific approach by reason of his human rather than avian purpose, namely, to shadow forth the classes in English society. Before turning to the lifeless bird list of Alanus, Chaucer thus imaginatively provides a guiding clue to his purpose in the *Parlement.*

Followed in this respect by the Elizabethan Michael Drayton, Alanus had represented birds as woven in the wonderful garments of Nature. More naturally, as Robinson remarks, "Chaucer represents them as gathered around the goddess" (p. 904). First is the eagle (331 ff.):

That with his sharpe lok perseth the sonne,
And othere egles of a lowere kynde,
Of whiche that clerkes wel devyse conne.

The poet commences by naming the most characteristic attribute of the eagle,[6] then for brevity refers the reader to the "clerkes," specialists like Pliny, for example, who, after Aristotle, describes six kinds of eagles (x. 3). As he then turns to Alanus, Chaucer, intimately familiar with falconry, elaborates the four chief species used in hunting. Whereas Alanus had merely named "the hawk," Chaucer draws upon familiar lore:

Ther was the tiraunt with his fetheres donne

"Quaedam comedunt carnem, quaedam grana, quaedam utrumque;
. . . quaedam vero comedunt vermes, ut passer. . . .
Vivunt et ex fructu quaedam aves, ut palumbi, et turtures.
Quaedam virunt in ripis aquarum lacuum, et cibantur ex eis."

[6] The sun-gazing eagle persisted until Milton's time. As quoted by Skeat (*ibid.*, p. 517), Vincent repeats Isidore's etymology: "*Aqu*-ila ab *ac*-umine oculorum vocata est."

And grey, I mene the goshauk, that doth pyne
To bryddes for his outrageous ravyne.
The gentyl faucoun, that with his feet distrayneth
The kynges hand; the hardy sperhauk eke,
The quayles foo; the merlioun, that payneth
Hymself ful ofte the larke for to seke; . . .

Chaucer's epithet "tiraunt" was suggested by Alanus' hawk, which "demanded tribute from its subjects with violent tyranny" (*tyrannide*), and this is the only reflection of Alanus in the passage.[7] Altogether each writer includes some thirty-odd birds, Chaucer naming eight omitted in Alanus, who mentions seven neglected in the *Parlement.* Chaucer depends also upon the encyclopedists, as in

The crane, the geaunt, with his trompes soun,

where size derives from Alanus and sound from Bartholomew or Vincent (xvi. 91), who quotes Isidore: "Quem

[7] Frequent hawking allusions denote Chaucer's familiarity with kinds and their prey. Compare, e.g., the distressed falcon found by Canacee, in the *Squire's Tale* (422–29):

"For ther nas nevere yet no man on lyve,
If that I koude a faucon wel discryve,
That herde of swich another of fairnesse,
As wel of plumage as of gentillesse
Of shap, of al that myghte yrekened be.
A faucon peregryn thanne semed she
Of fremde land."

Tyrwhitt has noted the accuracy of this etymology, quoting the *Trésor* of Brunetto Latini, "Des Faucons" (in Skeat's translation, p. 383): "The second kind is the falcon which is called the pilgrim (or peregrine), because no one ever finds its nest; but it is otherwise taken, as it were on *pilgrimage,* and is very easily fed, and very tame and bold, and well-mannered." Of the peregrine, or haggart: "She doth come from forayne partes a stranger and a passenger . . . as if a man would call them Pilgrims or Forayners." (G. Turberville, *Booke of Faulconrie,* 1575, pp. 26, 34.) Chaucer's last phrase, from a foreign country, denotes his knowledge of the peregrine's name and rarity as the earlier lines exactly describe the bird.

nomen de propria voce sumpserunt, tali enim sono susurrant." Chaucer's "theef the chough" reflects Alanus' adjective *latrocinio* (the Latin for "chough" is *monedula,* which the encyclopedists derived from *monetum tollere,* an etymology surviving in Gesner).

For Alanus' ravished Philomela Chaucer's is a more realistic bird (351):

That clepeth forth the grene leves newe.

As Skeat notes, this is reminiscent of Pliny's opening sentence describing the bird and its song (x. 43): "The song of the nightingale is to be heard, without interruption, for fifteen days and nights, continuously, when the foliage is thickening."[8]

Just as he always writes lovingly of the nightingale, so Chaucer always condemns the cuckoo, here "ever unkynde" —that is, of course, unnatural. Chaucer is in accord with Clanvowe and, it should be noted, with Neckam: "Thus, thus, nourishing in its breast the bitterness of a brother's hatred, it falls silent from divine praises; but afterwards, having surrendered to the thought of its tranquil life, it gladly opens its mouth in divine praises. . . . The cuckoo, tedious trifler in its futile repetition of its frequent note, sets forth the type of avarice, proclaiming and announcing, 'Give, give.' "[9] Chaucer's later nightingale passages will be noted below.

[8] *The Natural History of Pliny,* tr. Bostock and Riley (London, 1857), II, p. 509.

[9] "Sic, sic a laudibus divinis obmutescit rancorem fraterni odii quis nutriens in corde, sed postmodum tranquillitati vitae contemplativae deditus, hilariter os in laudes divinas aperit. . . . Cuculus frequenti eiusdem soni inutili repetitione taediosus nugator avaritiae typum gerit, proclamantis et

The heron is "the eles fo" (eel's foe); Alanus mentions the falcon as the heron's foe; to Vincent the stork (*ciconia*) is the enemy of snakes ("serpentium"), to Bartholomew the enemy of "Adders and Serpents," and to Neckam the enemy of frogs and crayfish ("ranarum et locustarum"). Later in Alanus the stork is called "the bird of concord," which, like Chaucer's drake, decimates its brood. In the stork as "wrekere of avouterye" Chaucer perpetuates the tradition repeated with variations by the encyclopedists. As it has been remarked, Neckam and Bartholomew, who cite Aristotle, state that this bird kills an unfaithful mate. In heraldry the stork was emblematic of gratitude both because the young care for the parents in age (see Figure 8) and because it blinds a human adulterer in gratitude to the husband who has rendered hospitality to the bird, a story found in Aelian (*De natura animalium,* viii. 20). Speght had suggested that "wrekere" should be rather "bewrayer." Thynne's comment illustrates the manner of explaining Chaucer by referring to the encyclopedists:

Whiche in truthe, accordinge to one propryete of his nature, may be as you saye, but accordinge to one other propryete of his nature, yt sholde bee "the wreaker of Adulterye," as Chaucer hath; for he ys a greater wreaker of the adulterye of his owne kynde and female, then the bewrayer of the adulterye of one other kynde, and of his hostesse, one the toppe of whose howse he harborethe, for Aristotle sayethe, and Bartholomeus de proprietatibus rerum li.12.cap.8 [Batman, p. 181r,v] with manye other auctors, that yf the storke by anye meanes perceve that his female hath brooked spousehedde, he will no more

dicentis, 'Affer, affer.' " (Alexander Neckam, *De naturis rerum libri duo,* ed. Thomas Wright, London, 1863, pp. 102, 117.)

dwell with her, but strykethe, and so cruelly beateth her, that he will not surcease vntill he hathe killed her yf he maye, to wreake and revenge that adulterye.[10]

Possibly the poet's haste or apathy in this unreal catalogue appears in his strangely designating the pheasant "skornere of the cok by nyghte." Alanus' nondescript pheasant is followed by the domestic cock, which divides the hours, after which appears the wild cock, "gallus silvestris, privatioris galli *deridens* desidiam," deriding the idleness of the domestic cock. Possibly, as Skeat notes, Chaucer has confused Alanus' pheasant with the wild cock. But Vincent (xvi. 72) writes, "Fasianus est gallus sylvaticus," or, as Skeat further surmises, "He may allude to the fact that the pheasant will breed with the common hen." Gilbert White describes a strange dead bird brought to him for identification. He concludes that it is a hybrid of a "cock pheasant and some kind of domestic fowl"; and he is so impressed that he has the bird painted—the only illustration appearing in *The Naturalist's Calendar.*[11] For Chaucer's line another equally reasonable explanation has been proposed: "Just as the cock, Chanticleer, crows at dawn, so the pheasant crows at sunset before he climbs to roost."[12]

[10] *Animadversions upon Speght's Chaucer,* ed. F. J. Furnivall (London, Chaucer Society, 1875), p. 68. In the *Gesta Romanorum,* 82, Christ is allegorized as the male stork, who punishes the impenitent, the guilty female.

[11] London, 1795, p. 68.

[12] "Bombardier," "Chaucer, Ornithologist," *Blackwood's Magazine,* CCLVI (August, 1944), p. 125. This author is wholly unaware of Chaucer's model in Alanus, believing that except for the hawks "all the other birds appear higgledy-piggledy according to the exigencies of metre or rhyme" (p. 121). A glance at Alanus' birds would have cleared up most of the puzzles for this writer, who concludes that "Chaucer was a good naturalist, or, at any rate, an uncommonly good observer" (p. 125). Pliny is the only authority recognized. Disregard "my boke and my devocioun" and the

By reason of this habit, perhaps, the pheasant is "scorner of the cock by night."

Deliberate transposition sometimes occurs, as in,

The raven wys; the crowe with vois of care.

Whereas Alanus endows the crow with the art of predicting, Chaucer gives the raven this wisdom. Alanus' raven, with biblical reminiscence (see Chapter IV, "Milton," page 103), disclaims its white fledglings until they grow black like itself. Skeat believes that, on the crow, Chaucer mistranslates, through Bartholomew's error, Vergil's line (*Geor.* i. 388),

Nunc plena cornix pluviam vocat improba voce.

Bartholomew's crow "calleth rayne with an eleinge voyce"; *improba* he translates in the sense of mournful or miserable rather than impudent or insulting. Chaucer's "care" means, of course, anxiety, hence ill luck.

Finally, to Alanus Chaucer adds two familiar English birds, the throstle and the fieldfare. The first he terms "old," possibly from the superstition mentioned by Swainson "that thrushes acquire new legs and cast the old ones, when about ten years old."[13] The fieldfare is termed "frosty" because, as the poet remembers, it appears in England only in the winter.[14]

---

necessity is to make of Chaucer more an ornithologist than a student of bird lore.

[13] *Provincial Names and Folk Lore of British Birds* (London, 1885), p. 4.

[14] Chaucer twice employs the proverb, "farewell, fieldfare." In the first (*Troilus and Criseyde* iii. 861),

"The harm is don, and far-wel feldefare"

the meaning is, as Skeat notes (*The Works of Chaucer,* II, p. 479), "when

All in all, Chaucer's method is to condense into a single word or phrase the full sentences of his original. With one elaboration, in the case of the hawks, and with occasional transpositions of attributes, Chaucer's catalogue faithfully and in pedestrian mood follows his Latin text. One critic believes he evinces greater originality in characterizing his birds.[15] On the contrary, Chaucer's variations from Alanus are usually to be noted in Neckam, Vincent, or Bartholomew. In this enumeration Chaucer is painting a background for the real matter of the poem. Alanus provided a ready catalogue with the usual human attributes, conventional and traditional, just as Vincent's classification from Aristotle served the earlier purpose in a poem where birds stand for people. Thus Chaucer's *Parlement* clearly reflects the medieval world picture in which the correspondencies are pointed out with traditional care. As a convention, the catalogue here subserves an artistic purpose, thus differing from the lifeless massing in his translation of the *Romaunt.*

In Chaucer generally, it may be observed, the despicable attributes of humanity most frequently suggest comparison with birds. Into this group fall twelve, or one-third, of the

---

an opportunity is missed, the harm is done; and people will cry, 'farewell, fieldfare' by way of derision, or 'the harm is done, and nobody cares.' " In the *Romaunt,* 5510,

"And synge, 'Go, fare-wel, feldefare' "

the reference is to false friends, who, when fortune frowns, say " 'Go! Farewell fieldfare,' i.e., Begone, we have done with you," as the departure of this winter bird is a welcome sign of approaching summer.

[15] Willard E. Farnham, "The Fowls in Chaucer's Parlement," *University of Wisconsin Studies in Language and Literature,* No. 2 (1918), pp. 340–66, especially p. 345.

birds in the *Parlement* list. The lecherous sparrow, "Venus sone" (*P.F.* 351) appears again in the *Summoner's Tale* (1804) with delicate suggestion,

And kiste hire sweete, and chirketh as a sparwe.

Even the swallow is a villain (*P.F.* 353–54):

mortherere of the foules smale
That maken hony of floures freshe of hewe

(the encyclopedias consistently classed bees with birds). Ominous ravens, crows, and owls, treacherous lapwings, cowardly kites, jangling jays and pies, murderous cuckoos, venomous shrikes ("waryangles"), ignorant geese, gluttonous cormorants, telltale starlings, thieving choughs—most of these epithets trace to the encyclopedists. Yet their application in Chaucer is always vivid if more true of his human than his avian subjects. And despite the nefarious ways of certain birds, Chaucer still conveys his own pleasure in recognizing their humanity.

Chaucer everywhere imparts to his verse his evident delight in outdoor pursuits and in the melodies of "smale foules." A survey of his poetry, accordingly, shows that the medieval manner of analogy disclosed in the imitative passage from the *Parlement* prevails, yet with a new and original touch. By means of the brief simile Chaucer lends color to his verse as these terse, apt comparisons instantly suggest human character, mannerism, or appearance. Though the prevailing characters of birds were deeply embedded in tradition, in the *Canterbury Tales* Chaucer is to some extent freed from the symbolism of the encyclopedia and has mastered the art of turning to his own ends the ancient lore of birds.

To human mood, posture, and action, birds contribute frequent analogy. Chaucer expresses carefreedom a few times by comparison with birds, as, for example, in the *Cook's Tale* (4367),

Gaillard he was as goldfynch in the shawe.

The magpie appears similarly several times: "stibourne and strong, and joly as a pie" (*Wife of Bath's Prologue* 456), "as jolif as a pye" (*Shipman's Tale* 1399), and "peert as is a pye" (*Reeve's Tale* 3950). The same role is twice applied to the popinjay (*Shipman's Tale* 1559; *Merchant's Tale* 2322). As a game bird, the bittern was known to him, though it is to the traditionally strange origin of the bird's cry that he refers. Disclosing to the reader the secret of her husband's asslike ears Midas' wife leans into the marsh (*Wife of Bath's Tale* 972),

As a bitoure bombleth in the myre.

Chaucer may have noticed the explanation in Bartholomew that the bittern puts its bill into the mud to produce its strange note.[16]

Chaucer combined learning with observation. In St. Jerome, as Skeat notes, he may have remembered the description of Jovinian as "formosus, crassus, nitidus, dealbatus,

[16] Of the miredromble, or "onacrotalus": it "putteth the bill doune into the water, and maketh a great noise" (p. 186v). This bird, "a kinde of cormorant," is regarded as separate from the bittern (*botaurus*), which Bartholomew names ("bitter") but does not describe. Chaucer rightly associates the manner of effecting its cry with the bittern. It took centuries to disprove this notion as well as another, equally fantastic—that the bird inserted its bill into a hollow reed (see Chapter V, "Drayton," p. 120).

et quasi sponsus semper incedens." But transforming these adjectives in the line (*Summoner's Tale* 1930)

Fat as a whale, and walkynge as a swan,

the poet presents a picture, immediate and graphic because familiar. Here observation derives from actual experience and hence instantly suggests two physical characteristics. Chaucer has thus gone beyond the imitative catalogue habit of the *Parlement,* where, with Alanus before him, he had merely repeated a familiar formula (*P.F.* 342),

The jelous swan, ayens his deth that syngeth.

Rarely does the reader encounter the extended simile, familiar in the Renaissance poems of Spenser. In the translation from Ovid (*Met.* vi. 529–30), Progne's fright is thus depicted (*Legend of Good Women* 2319–22):

Or as the culver, that of the egle is smiten,
And is out of his clawes forth escaped,
Yit is afered and awhaped,
Lest it be hent eft-sones; so sat she.

In a less imitative mood Chaucer would have dispensed with the simile in a swift phrase. Compare Criseyde as she protests her love (*Troilus and Criseyde* iii. 1495–98):

That first shal Phebus fallen fro his spere,
And everich egle ben the dowves feere . . .
Er Troilus out of Criseydes herte.[17]

[17] A French proverb (for parallels, see Robinson, *op. cit.,* p. 995) expressing the equally incredible appears in the *Romaunt* (4031–33),
"This have I herd ofte in seiyng,
That man may, for no dauntyng,
Make a sperhauk of a bosard."
That is, as Skeat explains (*The Works of Chaucer,* I, 436), "No man, by

Chaucer knew the tale of Philomela in Ovid and, including it in the *Legend of Good Women,* told it for its own sake as narrative. He declined to transfer to the bird the sadness of the ravished daughter of King Pandion. And in *Troilus,* recollections of the nightingale's actual timidity in its initial song provoked a striking simile (iii. 1233 ff.):

And as the newe abaysed nyghtyngale,
That stynteth first whan she bygynneth to synge,
Whan that she hereth any herde tale,
Or in the hegges any wyght stirynge,
And after siker doth hire vois outrynge,
Right so Criseyde, whan hire drede stente,
Opned hire herte, and tolde hym hire entente

"The art of attuning to the changing moods of Nature the passions of his characters so as to project them against a background of sympathetic natural scenery he might have learnt from Troilus," remarks Hayes, who notes in *Troilus* the elaborateness of simile and deplores its decline in the later poems.[18] The above lines are as eloquent of the hesitating woman as of the exact and often-remarked trials of voice peculiar to the nightingale. In the *Miller's Tale* the wooing parish clerk "syngeth, brokkynge as a nyghtyngale" (3377), that is, *quaveringly.* With the Renaissance the nightingale was to suffer a long eclipse as "she" wept her Ovidian fate; Milton was to revive its symbolic significance in the song drawn from Clanvowe's poem; and Coleridge was to restore the bird to its real status as an

taming it, can make a sparrow-hawk of a buzzard," for unlike the sparrow hawk, the buzzard was useless for hunting.

18 James Hayes, *The English Poet's Nature Lore: A Study in Chaucer* (Cork, 1917), p. 47.

exuberant *male.* But no poet was to observe the nightingale more keenly than Chaucer.

By and large, however, Chaucer's birds remain symbolic in their traditional character as patterns comparable with the infinite variety in human nature. His originality in this regard lies, not in anticipating the minute observation of later poets or in directing attention to the natural world for its own sake, but in transforming the world of the encyclopedia and employing its lore for graphic sketches of humankind. This he regards as the business of poetry, and however extensive his natural knowledge or his delight in the world of nature Chaucer does not forget this end. That Chaucer's art of drawing upon birds was not confined to the brief simile is evidenced in a concluding illustration. If, as William Turner later observed, "poets observe more negligently than philosophers," yet certain details from the Nun's Priest's barnyard prove the obverse as Chaucer transmutes lifeless untruths found in the encyclopedia of Bartholomew. At the outset the poet takes advantage by disclaiming all pretense of truth to nature. His triumph lies in leading the reader to forget that these protagonists are cock and hen, whereas his prototype, Bartholomew, solemnly describes what he believes to be authentic natural history.

Chaucer's royal figure of Chanticleer, too familiar to require quotation, owes his lineage to Bartholomew, whose hero "beareth a redde combe on his head in stade of a crowne."[19] His choleric complexion makes him "bolde and

[19] *Batman uppon Bartholome* . . . (London, 1582), p. 183. Beyond this royal suggestion the cock is no further described. One student believes that Chaucer's Gallic pair can be no other than Golden Spangled Hamburgs

hardie." "And so he fighteth boldly for his hennes[20] against his adversaries, . . . and when he hath the mastry he syngyth anon, and ere he syngyth he beateth himselfe with his wings to make him the more able to sing." In vanity, not victory,

This Chauntecleer his wynges gan to bete,
As man that koude his traysoun not espie,
So was he ravysshed with his flaterie.

Chaucer's hero has been betrayed by his own pride and by Venus. However cogent his wife's realistic reference to dreams and however bitter the herbs, more bitter are her taunts of cowardice. These are more reminiscent of Bartholomew's Capon, who "is more coward of heart than the Cocke" (p. 184). Actually Chanticleer thrusts aside his own true presentiments, caught in the lure of Venus and of pride. Woman is man's joy and all his bliss, but woe, that latter end of joy, overtakes the husband who accepts her "conseils." Freely using the epic of Reynard, Chaucer has deliberately reversed the attitudes of the main characters toward dreams.[21] Thus logically the butt of the poet's light-hearted satire is not only woman but also in this case herb lore, which, on the basis of her skepticism, rashly leads her spouse to defy "both sweven and dreem." But with equal

(Lalia P. Boone, "Chauntecleer and Partlet Identified," *Modern Language Notes,* LXIV, 1949, pp. 78–81).

20 The translation of Berthelet (1535), p. clxxv, r, consistently reads *wyves.* Batman continues: "And in fighting he smiteth the ground with his bill, and reareth up the feathers about his necke, to make him the more bold & hardy, and mooveth the feathers of his tayle upwarde and downwarde, that he may so the more ably come to the battaile."

21 "The French cock comes to grief because he will not accept his wife's advice; the English cock comes to grief because he does accept it." (J. Burke Severs, "Chaucer's Originality in the 'Nun's Priest's Tale,' " *Studies in Philology,* XLIII, 1946, p. 29.)

University of Texas Library

4. Cocks fighting. (From Johann von Cube, *Hortus Sanitatis,* Mainz, 1491, fol. 315[a].)

deliberation Chaucer again shifts attention away from Partlet's false counsel to the real cause of Chanticleer's fall—his vanity and voluptuousness. For certain hints in this carefully wrought structure, again Bartholomew may have been responsible.

Bartholomew now explains the cock's marital relations: "And he loveth derely his wyves . . . and he setteth next to him on the rooste, the hen that is most fat and tender, and loveth hir best, & desireth most to have hir presence." In the *Roman de Renart,* it will be recalled, Pinte is the wife favored because she lays the largest eggs.[22] Dame Partlet holds Chanticleer's heart "loken in every lith" because she is "the faireste hewed on hir throte," yet only Bartholomew and Chaucer allude to her place of honor:

As Chauntecleer among his wives alle
Sat on his perche, that was in the halle,
And next hym sat this faire Pertelote, . . .

Stinting their differences and speaking of mirth as morning breaks, Chanticleer woos his mate with lavish attention:

For whan I feele a-nyght your softe syde,
Al be it that I may nat on yow ryde. . . .
. . . I diffye both sweven and dreem.
And with that word he fley down fro the beem,
For it was day, and eke his hennes alle,
And with a chuk he gan hem for to calle,
For he hadde founde a corn, lay in the yerd.
Real he was, he was namoore aferd.
He fethered Pertelote twenty tyme,
And trad hire eke as ofte, er it was pryme.

The heart of this passage may be perceived in Bartholo-

22 "Celle qui les gros hues ponnoit." (*Sources and Analogues of Chaucer's Canterbury Tales,* ed. Bryan and Dempster, Chicago, 1941, p. 648.)

mew's drab prose: "In the morrow tide when he flyeth to get his meate, first he layeth his side to hir side, and by certain tokens and beckes, as it were love taches, he wooeth and prayeth hir to treading. . . . The Cocke he searcheth his meate with his bill and foote . . . and when hee findeth a grayne, he calleth, and cackeleth to him his Hens."

It would be difficult to discover whence Bartholomew derived his barnyard lore. Nevertheless, after the long efforts to discover the origins of Chaucer's *Nun's Priest's Tale,* whether French or German, it would be gratifying to know that for some features he turned to Bartholomew the Englishman.

In so far as the theme of birds is concerned, Chaucer's evolution as artist follows a fairly marked pattern. He begins with the translation of the *Romaunt of the Rose,* which comprises only enumeration without imaginative purpose. As this habit is carried over into the *Parlement,* where the poet follows Alanus, the advance is marked by several changes. First, he employs the Aristotelian classification of birds to represent social classes as preparation for satire. Then, before enumerating his avian company, he represents its members as grouped about Nature instead of as inanimate figures woven in a garment. Finally in *The Canterbury Tales* themselves the poet emerges as master of the concise simile, in which birds play a major role. The poet's interest in swift narrative precludes the extended simile inherited by the Renaissance writer of epic. The natures of birds had been fixed through the centuries of bestiary and encyclopedia. Chaucer's most ambitious attempt to apply bird nature to human nature is, as has been seen, in the entire conception of the *Nun's Priest's Tale.* Chaucer's use of avian figures is always medieval in manner in that birds are introduced symbolically. What distinguishes his later from his earlier work in this regard is his growing use of swift simile to depict character for its own sake. The objective artist thus supplants the moralist; yet for both, the world of birds provides examples of human character and action.

III : *Spenser*

WRITING OF THE ELIZABETHANS and looking forward rather than backward, Sir Edmund Chambers thus describes their outlook upon nature:

There is none of that accurate observation which Darwin has taught our modern poets, any more than there is that haunting sense of immanent Deity which they have inherited from Wordsworth. . . . Nature for them was a thing only to be felt, not studied; emotion was its interpreter and not science. They caught the fresh innocent delight of childhood and were content to miss the subtler, if not higher, pleasures which come of greater knowledge and understanding.[1]

Chaucer too, imitative as he was, shared this greater knowledge and understanding. Yet even as the Renaissance stumbled over the earlier pentameter, so it could hardly have been expected to affect the semiserious manner in which Chaucer turned to his purpose the symbolic lore of the Middle Ages. Unaware of his peculiar realism and mindful of the new god Decorum, Spenser was content to acknowledge Chaucer as his Tityrus, the well of English undefiled, who taught him "homely as I can to make" without ever capturing the actual mood or method of his master. His poetic theory being more like Vergil's, when Spenser followed his professed master he did so deliberately and openly; there is little evidence of assimilation. With regard to natural history, the gulf separating the realistic Chaucer from Spenser is well illustrated in their allusions to caged birds. Comparison of these passages will serve to introduce the systematic review of Spenser's verse.

As in the *Squire's Tale,* where a gently born tercelet becomes enamoured of a kite and Chaucer is reminded of the natural instinct of birds to escape the cage for the wood (611–20), so also in the *Manciple's Tale,* Phoebus' wife is false with "a man of litel reputacioun" (Phoebus' white crow discloses her infidelity and as a result is bereft of white feathers and song) (160–74):

But God it woot, ther may no man embrace

[1] *English Pastorals* (London, 1895), pp. xli–xlii.

As to destreyne a thyng which that nature
Hath natureelly set in a creature.
  Taak any bryd, and put it in a cage,
And do al thyn entente and thy corage
To fostre it tendrely with mete and drynke
Of alle deyntees that thou kanst bithynke,
And keep it al so clenly as thou may,
Although his cage of gold be never so gay,
Yet hath this brid, by twenty thousand foold,
Levere in a forest, that is rude and coold,
Goon ete wormes and swich wrecchednesse.
For evere this brid wol doon his bisynesse
To escape out of his cage, yif he may.
His libertee this brid desireth ay.

This passage suggests a bent of mind which two centuries later was to express itself in scientific observation. In writing of caged birds the poet was concerned with what "nature hath natureelly set in a creature": in the world of birds and other animals as in that of man, the compelling instincts are not to be denied. The nightingale passage from *Troilus* is striking because it is both lyrically beautiful and scientifically exact. The nightingale is a bird whose manner of song Chaucer has keenly observed. Both illustrations he introduces, not for their own sake, but as cogent aids in expressing objectively human nature and human emotion; yet in neither is there violence to the actual world of birds.

This approach, direct and realistic, contrasts strongly with the romantic feeling of Spenser's sonnet (*Amoretti,* LXV):

The doubt which ye misdeeme, fayre love, is vaine,

That fondly feare to loose your liberty,
When loosing one, two liberties ye gayne,
And make him bond that bondage earst dyd fly.
Sweet be the bands the which true love doth tye,
Without constraynt or dread of any ill:
The gentle birde feeles no captivity
Within her cage, but singes and feeds her fill . . .
There Fayth doth fearlesse dwell in brasen towre,
And spotlesse Pleasure builds her sacred bowre.

Again in LXXIII, the poet's heart flies to his lady:

. . . Like as a byrd, that in ones hand doth spy
Desired food, to it doth make his flight.
Even so my hart, that wont on your fayre eye
To feed his fill, flyes backe unto your sight.
Doe you him take, and in your bosome bright
Gently encage, that he may be your thrall:
Perhaps he there may learne, with rare delight,
To sing your name and prayses over all,
That it hereafter may you not repent,
Him lodging in your bosome to have lent.

Whether birds do respond to human kindness is obviously irrelevant to Spenser's aim, which is to enlist the similes as conceits addressed to his mistress. For him the criterion is poetic excellence, not the relationship of birds to their habitat; and once this is admitted, the reader is prone to forget the violence to nature. Feeling has now become the medium through which nature filters into verse.

In a survey of Spenser's birds it appears that almost solely in the epic simile, where Spenser enters the familiar province of falconry, does Decorum coincide with observation. Throughout *The Shepheardes Calender* the world of nature is always "a myrrhour to behold my plight." And as the external world reflects the poet's mood, so with equal deliberation the mood is attuned to the season. The naked winter trees of January induce sadness in the recollection of the leafy months of summer, when "birds were wont to build their bowre." In March the signs of spring appear, and (11)

The Swallow peepes out of her nest.

Jusserand quite misconstrues this line to the poet's discredit: "On croirait . . . que les hirondelles se cachent dans leurs nids l'hiver et sortent la tête au printemps. . . ."[2] But actually Renaissance science supported the residence of swallows in their nests during winter. Spenser may have noted Gesner's experience with swallows:

I have heard of swallows concealed in the nest in winter as if dead; accordingly I do not believe that they depart. With them for the entire winter they cherish their eggs fresh; moreover, the swallows come to life again in summer's warmth. Wherefore I declare that this performance is in some degree marvelous and a symbol of the resurrection of our bodies.[3]

Gesner's conclusion also fully accords with Spenser's sym-

[2] *A Literary History of the English People* (3 vols., London, 1906), II, p. 408.

[3] "Comperi latere hieme hirundines in nido suo tamquam mortuas; proinde non puto avolare eas. Totam hiemem habent secum recentia ova, reviviscunt autem sub aestatem. Quare indico mirabile quoddam opus esse, ac imaginem resurrectionis nostrorum corporum." (Gesner, *De avium natura*, Zurich, 1555, p. 529.) Cf. Abraham Cowley, *Anacreontics* (1656) on the swallow:

"In thy undiscover'd nest
Thou dost all the winter rest,
And dreamest o'er thy summer joys
Free from the stormy season's noise. . . ."

bolic outlook. On the other hand, the poet may intend here only to suggest the sight of an incubating swallow as one of the signs of the season, or, as "E. K." makes clear, "which bird useth to be counted the messenger, and as it were, the forerunner, of springe." The choice is between books and observation, yet Spenser is capable of combining these (see Figure 2).

December, Spenser's adaptation of Marot's *Eglogue au Roy,* further typifies the English poet's manner. With a perceptible loss of Marot's sincerity and spontaneity, the rejected lover closes the series by reviewing the various seasonal occupations. With studied pretense he paraphrases the aging Marot, who had appealed to the king for aid. Lines 31 and 32,

O quantes fois aux arbres grimpé j'ay
Pour desnicher ou la pye ou le geay. . . .

are adapted thus:

How oft have I scaled the craggie oke,
All to dislodge the raven of her nest!

Spenser's generalizing tendency, to which further reference will be made, is apparent in lines superadded to his model (67–72):

Where I was wont to seeke the honey be,
Working her formall rowmes in wexen frame,
The grieslie todestoole growne there mought I se,
And loathed paddocks lording on the same:[4]
And where the chaunting birds luld me a sleepe,
The ghostlie owle her grievous ynne doth keepe.

[4] In the next century Spenser is here credited with a bit of exact observation (John Guillim, *A Display of Heraldrie,* 1611, p. 150): "*Toades* and

The *Complaints* poems reflect Spenser's habit of retrospection, noted in the contrasting passage from *December,* of mourning the present by comparing it with the happy past. Not infrequently it is voiced in terms of avian imagery (*The Ruines of Time* 127–33):

Where my high steeples whilom usde to stand,
On which the lordly faulcon wont to towre,[5]
There now is but an heap of lyme and sand,
For the shriche-owle to build her balefull bowre:
And where the nightingale wont forth to powre
Her restles plaints, to comfort wakefull lovers,
There now haunt yelling mewes and whining plovers.

Inevitably Philomel assumes her characteristic role in the sad comparison of the changing seasons with the desolated state of the arts (*Teares of the Muses* 235–46):

Like as the dearling of the summers pryde,
Faire Philomele, when winters stormie wrath
The goodly fields, that earst so gay were dyde
In colours divers, quite despoyled hath,
All comfortlesse doth hide her chearlesse head.

So we, that earst were wont in sweet accord
All places with our pleasant notes to fill,
Whilest favourable times did us afford
Free libertie to chaunt our charmes at will,

Frogs do communicate this naturall property, that when they sit, they hold their heads steady & without motion: which stately action, *Spencer* in his *Shepheardes Calender* calleth the *Lording* of *Frogs*." (*The Short-title Catalogue* lists editions in 1610, 1611, 1632, and 1638.)

[5] Often in Spenser (*F.Q.* vi. x. 6) and always in Chaucer, the hawks, like the eagle, were put at the top of the scale. Cf. Chaucer (*P.F.* 323–24),

"the foules of ravyne
Weere hyest set, and thanne the foules smale."

Bodleian Library

Library of Congress

"The hoars night-raven, trump of dolefull dreare."
(Spenser, *Faerie Queene,* 1590)

5. (*Above*) Traditional night raven, or goatsucker. (From Johann von Cube, *Hortus Sanitatis,* Mainz, 1491, fol. 306[b].) (*Below*) True night raven, or black-crowned night heron. (From C. Gesner, *De avium natura,* Zurich, 1555, p. 603.)

All comfortlesse upon the bared bow,
Like wofull culvers, do sit wayling now.[6]

Here the nightingale hides her head before winter's wrath; so we (hide our heads), but (like culvers) we wail. But culvers have only a mournful note, summer and winter; the nightingale, silent after summer, has "hidden his head" in migration, as the author of *The Owl and the Nightingale* knew better than Spenser, who probably gave little thought to the questions of hibernation and migration. The above passage, telescoping similes as poetic filling, is another example of the common "where-once-see-now" convention. Its triteness contrasts with the acute observation in Chaucer's *Troilus* (iii. 1233 ff.) describing the fearful Criseyde.

To suggest desolation by grouping together various birds of ill omen is perhaps Spenser's most characteristic manner of introducing them. Hobbinol describes the bleak hills of northern England in terms of night ravens "more black than pitche," elvish ghosts, and "gastly owles" (*June* 23–24), which again "E. K." interprets: "By such hateful byrdes, hee meaneth all misfortunes (whereof they be tokens) flying every where." Such symbolic generalizations, frequent in Spenser,[7] differ strikingly from the

[6] Cf. *Amoretti* (LXXXVIII), in his mistress' absence,

"Like as the culver on the bared bough
Sits mourning for the absence of her mate."

According to Bartholomew, the lecherous culver nesting in rocks is distinct from the chaste turtle (see Index).

[7] For example, "banefull byrdes, whose shrieking sound/Ys signe of dreery death" (*August* 173–74); "fowle goblins and shriek-owles" (*Teares of the Muses* 282); the sea birds are "yelling Mewes and whining Plovers" (*Ruines of Time* 133), and "yelling Meawes, with Seagulles hoarse and bace,/And Cormoyrants, with birds of ravenous race" (*F.Q.* ii. xii. 8).

equally symbolic but particularized comparisons of Chaucer, whose characters are depicted in terms of the traditional pattern in nature.[8] In the marriage song Spenser is at fault in regard to the stork (*Epithalamion* 345–46):

Let not the shrieck oule, nor the stork be heard
Nor the night raven that still deadly yels, . . .

The stork, remarks D'Arcy Thompson, is "all but voiceless, and (save for a rare whimpering note) only clatters or 'clappers' with its bill."[9] Ovid uses the phrase "crepitante rostro" (*Met.* vi. 97). Renwick suggests that Spenser may be thinking of Lucretius' "grum clamor" (noise of cranes) or of Ovid's *strix* (little owl) (*Met.* vii. 269). "It is not that Spenser translated thus, but 'stryx' may have been at the back of his mind along with the other unlucky night-birds, and 'stork' is the impressionistic result."[10] Perhaps the poet knew no distinction between the voiceless stork and the loud cranes and herons. Furthermore, the owls were identified, not with storks, even impressionistically, but with night ravens, which Spenser now adds.

One group of ominous, "obscene" birds in the *Faerie Queene* is the subject of extensive comment by Robinson.[11] On their way to the Bower of Bliss, Guyon and Palmer are

8 Rarely does Spenser adopt the Chaucerian manner of individually symbolic analogy. From Alciati (Emblem 90) or Aristotle (*Ethics* iii. 10), he compares the neck of Gluttony to that of a crane (*F.Q.* i. iv. 21) and presents Disdaine "stalking stately like a crane" (*F.Q.* vi. vii. 42) (see Figure 11). See *Works of Edmund Spenser,* variorum ed. (9 vols., Baltimore, Johns Hopkins Press, 1932–49), I, p. 219.

9 D'Arcy W. Thompson, *A Glossary of Greek Birds* (Oxford, 1895), p. 70.

10 *Works of Edmund Spenser, Minor Poems,* II, pp. 486–87.

11 Phil Robinson, *The Poets' Birds* (London, 1883), p. 386. The author's excesses and errors are pointed out in a review, "A Literary Curiosity," *Atlantic Monthly,* LIV (1884), pp. 398–413.

encompassed by evil, which is symbolized thus (*F.Q.* ii. xii. 36):

And fatall birds about them flocked were,
Such as by nature men abhorre and hate,
The ill-faste owl, death's dreadfull messengere,
The hoars night-raven, trump of dolefull dreare,
The lether-winged batt, dayes enimy,
The ruefull strich, still waiting on the bere,
The whistler shrill, that who so heares doth dy,
The hellish harpyes, prophets of sad destiny.

"It is a delightful stanza," writes Robinson, "and I would not spare a word from it. It may not be exactly true that men 'naturally abhor and hate owls, or ravens either; that 'screech-owls' feed on human corpses, or that bats are birds—and whether there are such birds as 'whistlers' and 'harpyes' I do not care to consider, for the stanza is admirable as poetry, and epitomises every one of the poet's faults with regard to nature." In a footnote the author adds: "It illustrates (line 2) the apparent want of sympathy with nature that can suppose 'abhorrence' of owls *natural* to us; (lines 3 and 4) their [poets'] prejudice against special birds; (line 5) their errors of fact; (line 6) their habit of using a second name for a bird already utilised under another; (line 7) their invention of birds to eke out an adequate repertory, and (line 8) their candid enlistment of the fauna of fable" (p. 386). Similarly, "The poet's vulture has three aspects—as a bird of prey (which it is not), a bird of ill omen (which it was not), and a bird of general horror (which it should never be to poets)" (p. 466).

This criticism is filled with quibbling and misconstruc-

Folger Shakespeare Library

"And fatall birds about them flocked were,
Such as by nature men abhorre and hate."
(Spenser, *Faerie Queene,* 1590)

6. Group of nocturnal birds—goatsucker, owls, and bats. (From Olaus Magnus, *Historia de gentibus septentrionalibus* . . . , Rome, 1555, p. 692.)

tion. By "men" Spenser obviously means people generally, not scientists; and through the centuries people have hated night birds with their weird notes, among them the fearful "night raven" as well as the common raven. All the best authorities, Belon and Gesner for example, include the bat among birds. To the generic *owl* Spenser adds the "strich," remembering, from Gesner perhaps, that Latin *strix* was different from *bubo, noctua,* and other owls; and "waiting on" simply means "lingering near" in expectation of imminent death, not the nonsense of feeding upon cadavers. Whistler and night raven were real birds, though there was no general agreement about their other names in the long tradition of omen. As elsewhere it has been suggested, the first name was often applied to one of the curlews, the second to the night raven and to the nightjar, European member of the goatsucker family.[12] Harpies, as the poet knew, were fabulous; their nature and history he could learn from Gesner (iii, pp. 524–26). Thus Spenser's stanza is redolent of the long tradition enveloping those birds grouped by Belon as "oiseaux de nuict," and by Olaus Magnus as "aves nocturni" (see Figure 6). Stressing the horror of their presence, Olaus names five kinds of owls—bubo, otis, ulula, noctua, and strix—bats, and goatsuckers, and the woodcut embodies these birds in spirit as in kind. Spenser closely follows suit in the quoted stanza.

Thus, in the poet's thinking, science merges with folklore. Mere names can be redolent of ill omen; as "ensamples" they carry on the "doctrine" thus made explicit by cogent suggestion, and by very numbers the birds enhance the effect of intended evil. In the present consideration of birds as they appear in epic simile, it will be seen that Spenser pursues the identical purpose but with different effect. Depending upon Bartholomew only occasionally, the poet relies more upon his own experience in the field with falcons. As firsthand knowledge replaces or supplements that drawn from books, the effect is new and startling. That theory and practice are at variance will be

12 Thomas P. Harrison, "The Whistler, Bird of Omen," *Modern Language Notes,* LXV (1950), pp. 39–41; and "Two of Spenser's Birds: Nightraven and Tedula," *Modern Language Review,* XLIV (1949), pp. 232–35.

plain after a review of epic simile and its underlying theory.

Spenser employs the extended simile frequently and with realistic effect, if not always with exact analogy throughout. Of these similes the ones pertaining to falconry are most frequent and impressive. As Pauline Henley remarks: "The aristocratic position of hawking may have provided relaxation for his leisured moments, for Ireland of the period was famous for its hawks, which were valued so highly that they were sent as gifts to princes and nobles."[13] Spenser's knowledge of this sport is the more significant in view of the absence of imitation from Tasso and Ariosto, though there is some evidence of the poet's familiarity with Ovid and Vergil. Important links with Bartholomew appear. Still, in the simile drawn from falconry Spenser is uniquely at home: this is the one province of bird lore in which books take second place.

The first examples, from the *Faerie Queene,* depict the helpless victim of the hawk. Braggadochio, saved from Belphoebe's arrow by his squire, crawls from hiding (ii. iii. 35–36):

Forth creeping on his caitive hands and thies,
And standing stoutly up, his loftly crest
Did fiercely shake, and rowse, as coming late from rest.
As fearefull fowle, that long in secret cave
For dread of soring hauke, her selfe hath hid,
Not caring how, her silly life to save,

[13] *Spenser in Ireland* (London, 1928), pp. 95–96. Peregrines especially were collected from Irish eyries for English falconers, according to E. A. Armstrong. For commentary on Spenser's poetic effects, cf. Grace W. Landrum, "Images in the *Faerie Queene* Drawn from Flora and Fauna," *Shakespeare Association Bulletin,* XVI (1941), pp. 89–101, 131–39.

She her gay painted plumes disorderid,
Seeing at last her selfe from daunger rid,
Peepes forth and soone renews her native pride;
She gives her feathers fowle disfigured
Prowdly to prune, and sett on every side;
So shakes off shame, ne thinks how erst she did her hide.

This passage, writes Jack,[14] shows how Spenser's similes "elucidate what they are designed to illustrate," in this case Braggadochio's shameful cowardice, which emerges despite a pretended front of fierce pride. The poet's imagery here suggests Bartholomew's account of the culver, which "maketh his neast in dennes and holes of stones. He seeth the shadow of the Goshawke comming, and . . . flyeth into the inner place of an hoale, and there hideth it selfe. . . . [When her young] are borne away, she forgetteth hir harme and damage" (p. 180v). Spenser has other associations with the culver, forlorn and solitary after the loss of its mate; so to avoid weakening the comparison, the poet (if he does recall this passage) substitutes "fearefull fowle." Still, the craven pretense of his braggart—and this is the point of the episode of the bush—is lost in the comparison where the poet's implicit sympathy for the hunted bird tends to deny the equation of bird and braggart. Accordingly, even aside from Bartholomew's culver, the simile remains somewhat inept.

Happier is the simile in the picture of Florimell in her flight from Arthur, whom she mistakes for an enemy (iii. iv. 49):

[14] A. A. Jack, *A Commentary on the Poetry of Chaucer and Spenser* (Glasgow, 1920), p. 349. Cf. Jeremiah 48:28: "Leave the cities, and dwell in the rock, and be like the dove that maketh her nest in the sides of the hole's mouth."

But nothing might relent her hasty flight, . . .
Like as a fearefull dove, which through the raine
Of the wide ayre her way does cut amaine,
Having farre off espyde a tassell gent,
Which after her his nimble winges doth straine,
Doubleth her hast for feare to bee forhent,
And with her pineons cleaves the liquid firmament.
With no lesse hast, and eke with no lesse dreed, . . .

The last line draws attention to the double correspondence. Here Spenser perhaps remembers Vergil, who compares the effortless flight of the dove to that of a boat cleaving the water on the final stretch of a race: "Even as, if startled from her cave, a dove . . . wings her flight to the fields and, frightened from her home, flaps loudly with her wings; soon, gliding in the peaceful air, she skims her liquid way and stirs not her swift pinions" (*Aen.* v. 213–17).[15]

Another simile depicting the fearful victim at the mercy of its captor suggests Chaucer. Arthur wrestles Pyrochles to ground (ii. viii. 50):

Nought booted it the Paynim then to strive;
For as a bittur in the eagles clawe,
That may not hope by flight to scape alive,
Still waytes for death with dread and trembling aw,
So he, now subject to the victours law,
Did not once move, nor upward cast his eye,
For vile disdaine and rancour, which did gnaw
His hart in twaine with sad melancholy,
As one that loathed life, and yet despysed to dye.

[15] *Virgil,* tr. Rushton Fairclough (2 vols., Cambridge, Loeb Classical Library, 1937), I, p. 461.

Dishonored by Tereus, Chaucer's fearful Progne is thus described (*Legend of Good Women* 2319–22):

Or as the culver, that of the egle is smiten,
And is out of his clawes forth escaped,
Yit it is afered and awhaped,
Lest it be hent eft-sones; so sat she.

Spenser would also remember the corresponding lines in Ovid (*Met.* vi. 529–30).

A later episode again presents the ever-pursued Florimell in falconry terms. Thus inevitably—perhaps naturally—the poet's sympathy lies with the hunted rather than the hunter. Delivered from one enemy, the lady now confronts another supposed peril (iii. viii. 33):

Her selfe not savëd yet from daunger dredd
She thought, but chaung'd from one to other feare;
Like as a fearefull partridge, that is fledd
From the sharpe hauke, which her attached neare,
And fals to ground, to seeke for succor theare,
Whereas the hungry spaniells she does spye,
With greedy jawes her ready for to tere;
In such distresse and sad perplexity
Was Florimell, when Proteus she did see thereby.

Chaucer had named "the hardy sperhauk eke,/The quayles foo" (*P.F.* 339–40), and Bartholomew had well described the habits of the partridge (p. 187r):

He is feeble of flight, and in flight he riseth but little from the ground, and falleth oft to the ground after a little while. Also the Partridge dreadeth the Sparhauk, and flieth her: and as long as hee seeth the Sparhauke in the aire, he riseth not from the earth into the aire.

Jack is critical (p. 347): "Spenser does not often drag in a simile that is not suggested by the flow of imagination started by the context." He regards the above comparison as a lapse, "a mere turning aside to speak, as carefully as Spenser does, of the bird that, seeking cover from the hawk, falls a prey to the 'hungry spaniells.' " In his *Booke of Faulconrie* (1575) Turberville describes this device of the falconer, which he terms "a conspiracye (as it were) betwixt the dogges and Hawkes." Reference to this manual does not remove Jack's stricture; it *does,* however, show the accuracy of the poet's observation of an actual practice. Larks and small fowls are the game (p. 54):

> Finding themselves pursued by the hounds and spanels, (they) are enforst to trust to their wings, and to take the ayre; and being there, finding themselves molested by the Falconers and Hobbies, do make their choyse and election to become a pray rather to the dogs, or seeke mercy among the horse legges, and so to be surprised alive, then to affie to the curtesie of the cruell Hobbies, and to be taken in their cruell talons, where they are most assured to dye the death.

So great is their fear of the hobby that larks may be taken on the ground with snare or net. Merely holding the hawk up to view paralyzes the lark, a practice which Turberville compares to the "daring" of larks, "a very good sporte and full of delight to see the fearefull nature of the sillie Larcke, with the great awe and subiection that the Hobbie hath him in."

Spenser once alludes to this tactic. Diana and her attendants capture the spying Faunus (vii. vi. 47) by surrounding him. They

Enclos'd the bush about, and there him tooke,
Like darred larke, not daring up to looke
On her whose sight before so much he sought.

Apparently Turberville considered the practice too well known to warrant description. Under *dare,* meaning "to fascinate or paralyse with fear," the *NED* quotes a description of a daring glass as "a circular board with pieces of looking-glass inserted." These were used to bring to earth the flying bird or to freeze those on the ground for capture in nets. Often the hobby replaced the mirror to bring the birds down for capture with net, snare, or spaniels. Unlike the Florimell-partridge simile, Spenser's analogy here is not only limited but definitely contradictory. The terrified Faunus, like the lark, is captured. Spenser prefers the pun, however, to further analogy: Faunus *dares* not "up to looke on her whose sight before so much he sought." Fascination, not shame, overwhelms the bird.

Occasionally Spenser introduces resisting victims rather than the more usual helpless ones. In the climactic struggle of the First Book, the Dragon "with his broad sayles," having snatched up both rider and horse, soon is forced (i. xi. 19):

To let them downe before his flightles end:
As hagard hauk, presuming to contend
With hardy fowle, above his hable might,
His wearie pounces all in vaine doth spend
To trusse the pray too heavy for his flight;
Which, comming down to ground, does free it selfe by fight.

The poet's simile concludes with the imminence of a fight between hawk and "hardie fowle" as the two touch earth, and in this suggestion he anticipates the similar struggle now to follow as the knight turns upon his antagonist:

He so disseizëd of his gryping grosse,
The knight his thrillant speare againe assayd
In his bras-plated body to embosse,
And three mens strength unto the stroake he layd.

In this proleptic awareness, suggesting within the concluded simile the later course in major narrative, Spenser matches the more deliberate art of Milton (whose Satan, incidentally, was in part drawn from Spenser's dragon; see page 99, n. 21). Such prolepsis the earlier poet rarely achieved, for if within the simile itself the correspondencies do not fail, with its conclusion Spenser usually terminates abruptly the comparison with the ensuing narrative.

The second, and final, simile concerns falcons flying at the most prized and most difficult of game, the heron. It occurs in the final book at a moment when Arthur is set upon by two strange knights (vi. vii. 9):

As when a cast of faulcons make their flight
At an herneshaw, that lyes aloft on wing,
The whyles they strike at him with heedlesse might,
The warie foule his bill doth backward wring;
On which the first, whose force her first doth bring,
Her selfe quite through the bodie doth engore,
And falleth downe to ground like senselesse thing,
But th' other, not so swift as she before,
Fayles of her souse, and passing by doth hurt no more.

"Only a poet with his eyes on his object could have written this stanza," exclaims one critic.[16] Both the effectiveness of

[16] B. E. C. Davis, *Spenser, A Critical Study* (London, 1933), p. 175.

the simile and its background in falconry invite comment. In the narrative Prince Arthur has dispatched one attacker and now overcomes the second, who has returned. The lordly falcons correspond to the two miscreants, the heronshaw to the Prince, who, like the bird habitually, is at the moment on the defensive. Spenser thus concentrates attention upon the action, not upon the nature of the actors.

The simile itself derives possibly from observation, more likely from books, for actually a flying heron could hardly turn its bill backward. But the authorities were unanimous about this as a deliberately defensive act. In his *Art of Falconry,* Emperor Frederick II (1194–1250), the greatest of all medieval authorities on birds, writes: "The heron's most frequent refuge is water, and in flight she sometimes strikes with her beak. The crane, however, uses its talons and feet to lash out in the air at the attacking falcon."[17] The 1596 Latin edition of this great work exerted a considerable influence upon the literature of falconry, and possibly from this Bartholomew learned that "cranes when they knowe that the Falcon or the Goshawke commeth, they turne upward their bils, and defend themselves as well as they may, with sharpnesse of bill" (p. 183v). According to Turberville, both heron and crane were dangerous to the falconer's precious birds. In the training of hawks, herons, trapped or otherwise captured, were loosed, "after that you have brused both feete and bills" (p. 113). Sometimes the falconer used a captive heron "uppon the upper part of whose bill or truncke you must convey the ioynt of a reede or Cane,

[17] *The Art of Falconry: Being the de arte venandi cum avibus of Frederick II of Hohenstaufan,* tr. and ed. Casey A. Wood and F. Marjorie Fyfe (Stanford, Calif., Stanford University Press, 1943), p. 357.

How to flee the Hearon.

University of Texas Library

"As when a cast of faulcons make their flight
At an herneshaw, that lyes aloft on wing,
The whyles they strike at him with heedless might,
The warie foule his bill doth backward wring; . . ."
(Spenser, *Faerie Queene,* 1596)

7. A falconry scene. (From G. Turberville, *The Booke of Faulconrie,* 1575, p. 112.)

so as shee may not hurt the Hawke therewith" (p. 160). Then as the victim is borne to the earth, the falconer is urged: "Make in apace to reskew him [the hawk]; thrusting the Hearons bill into the grounde, breake his winges and legges that the Hawke may the more easily foote and plume it" (p. 162). Victim cranes should be similarly maimed "as they do the Hearnes, bycause they do Hawkes most wrong with their legges and feete" (p. 166). The woodcut in Turberville (see Figure 7) depicts a hawk trying to seize a heron, which, inverted in the air, fronts the enemy. In his *Animadversions upon Speght's Chaucer* (1598), Thynne elaborates Chaucer's "heroner" as (p. 39):

an especiall hawke (of anye of the kyndes of longe winged hawkes) of moore accompte then other hawkes are, because the flighte of the Herone ys moore dangerous then of other fowles, insomuche, that when she fyndethe her selfe in danger, she will lye in the ayre vppon her backe, and turne vpp her bellye towardes the hawke, and so defile her enemye with her excrementes, that eyther she will blinde the hawke, or ells with her byll or talentes pierce the hawkes brest, yf she offer to cease vppon her.[18]

[18] The word *heroner* occurs in *Troilus and Criseyde* (iv. 413) and *Legend of Good Women* (1120). For a later poetic version of the heroner's peril, cf. William Somerville, *Field Sports* (1742):

"Now like a wearied stag
That stands at bay, the hern provokes their [falcons'] rage
Close by his languid wing, in downy plumes,
Covers his fatal beak, and cautious hides
The well dissembled fraud. The falcon darts
Like lightning from above, and in her breast
Receives the latent death; down plumb she falls,
Bounding from earth, and with betrickling gore
Defiles her gaudy plumage. . . ."

Two similes are introduced to emphasize terrific impact, first of a victim struck by an eagle, then of a vulture which has missed its swoop. With his hand Arthur throws the crushed body of Maleger to the ground so forcefully (ii. xi. 42–43):

That back againe it did alofte rebound, . . .

As when Joves harnesse-bearing bird from hye
Stoupes at a flying heron with proud disdayne,
The stone-dead quarrey falls so forciblye,
That yt rebounds against the lowly playne,
A second fall redoubling back agayne.

Here the analogy ends, for Maleger, recovered,

Gan heap huge strokes on him, as ere he down was cast.

Diamond heaves an axe at Cambell, who dodges as his attacker almost falls (iv. iii. 19):

As when a vulture greedie of his pray
Through hunger long, that hart to him doth lend,
Strikes at an heron with all his bodies sway,
That from his force seemes nought may it defend;
The warie fowle, that spies him toward bend
His dredfull souse, avoydes it, shunning light,
And maketh him his wing in vaine to spend;
That with the weight of his owne weeldlesse might,
He falleth nigh to ground, and scarse recovereth flight.[19]

This seems to be Spenser's only serious lapse in naming the

[19] Cf. the preceding episode: Arthur returns to battle Maleger (ii. xi. 36):
"Eft fierce retourning, as a faulcon fayre,
That once hath failed of her souce full neare,
Remounts againe into the open ayre,
And unto better fortune doth her selfe prepayre."

birds of prey. As the vulture is a scavenger and depends solely upon carrion, the role of Spenser's bird is hardly a likely one. More appropriately in the *Epithalamion* (283) the poet includes "grieslie vultures" with the owl and other ominous birds. But Spenser has neglected Bartholomew, who reports (p. 188v,r): "The Vulture hath that name of slow flight, as Isidore sayeth. For of the plenteousnesse of much flesh, he lacketh swiftnesse of flight. . . . He getteth not lightly meat. . . . When he is alighted, unneth he riseth againe from the ground, as Gregory sayth." This last characteristic suggests Spenser's "scarse recovereth flight," and may have determined Spenser's choice of the vulture to illustrate this difficulty, which in the poem, however, proceeds from the force of his descent only.

The final instance of Spenser's resort to Bartholomew is clarified by the allegory, when arising from the well of life Red Cross is renewed like the eagle. Una witnesses the phenomenon (*F.Q.* i. xi. 34):

At last she saw, where he upstarted brave
Out of the well, wherein he drenched lay:
As eagle fresh out of the ocean wave,
Where he hath lefte his plumes all hory gray,
And deckt himselfe with fethers youthly gay,
Like eyas hauke up mounts unto the skies,
His newly budded pineons to assay,
And merveiles at him selfe, stil as he flies:
So new this new borne knight to battell new did rise.

Spenser's purpose coincides here with the *Physiologus*, where all the usual features of the well-known eagle transformation shadow man's salvation through rebirth in

Christ.[20] Batman's account, however, is suggestive: "In age the Eagle hath darknesse and dimnesse in eyen, and heavinesse in wings. And against this disadvantage she is taught by kinde, to seeke of a well of springing water, and then she flyeth up into the aire as farre as she may . . ." (p. 177r), and there undergoes renewal of both eyes and plumage. Spenser's eagle rose from "the ocean wave," his knight from "a springing well" (st. 39).

Earlier in the poem Spenser had compared Contemplation's "wondrous quick and persaunt spright" to "an eagles eie, that can behold the sunne" (i. x. 47), a common convention quoted by Bartholomew: "The Eagle is called Aquila and hath that name of sharpnesse of eyen, as Isidore sayth. . . . In the Eagle the spirit of sight is most temperate, and most sharpe in act and deede of seeing and beholding the Sunne in the roundnesse of his circle, without anye blemishing of eyen . . ." (p. 176v). Spenser would remember his English rendering of Du Bellay, appearing as *The Visions of Bellay,* where contradictorily, "the bird that can the sun endure" mounts the skies, falls in flames to the earth, and turns to ashes, from which (7),

> the foule that dothe the light dispise
> Out of her dust like to a worme arise.

Here the legends of eagle and phoenix are merged to symbolize in an emblem the transitoriness of human grandeur. With similar confusion in *The Visions of Petrarch* (5) the phoenix assumes the role of the traditional pelican in wounding itself with its bill. Woodcuts in Van der Noodt's earlier volume, in which Spenser's translations of Du Bel-

[20] Cf. *Works of Edmund Spenser, Minor Poems,* I, p. 303.

lay first appeared, present for the first emblem an eagle adjacent to the sun, below flames darting toward a falling bird, and on the earth a diminutive bird in a nest; and for the second emblem two birds, one wounding its bleeding breast. In so far as the emblem motif envelops the twelve poems of the *Calender,* decorum dictated inclusion of birds to symbolize the respective seasons as well as the human emotions appropriate to these seasons. Avian similes in Spenser's epic also symbolize human action, usually combat, and, less common than in Chaucer, human trait.

The student of these and other similes[21] from falconry may be reminded of the poet's Tristram (vi. ii. 32):

Ne is there hawke which mantleth her on pearch,
Whether high touring, or accoosting low,
But I the measure of her flight doe search,
And all her pray, and all her diet know.

Certainly Spenser is never closer to the life of his time than in such similes from the sport which his leisure must often have shared. When from the clear focus of these, the reader turns back to the narrative, he often finds himself in a phantom world. In attempting to follow the similes, "the imagination has nothing on which to stay itself before it passes on to the differences," as Elton remarks.[22] But for this failure, he continues, the similes "make amends, by their freshness and definition." Into them the poet infuses "the feeling and the humanity that are denied to most of his phantom knights and abstract women." Generally, writes Jack (p. 350), "the picture pre-

[21] Cf., e.g., *F.Q.* v. ii. 54; v. iv. 15; v. iv. 42.
[22] Oliver Elton, "Colour and Imagery in Spenser," *Modern Studies* (London, 1907), p. 75.

sented by the simile from observation is, for one reason or another, so much more attention-arresting, or so much grander, than the fancied event to which it is likened that one loses sight of the thing illustrated in admiration of the illustration."

However spontaneous this impression on the part of the modern reader it is likely that the poet himself would regard it as completely contrary to his intent. For what, after all, is the basic purpose in these similes comparing avian struggles aloft with those of doubted knights or with flight of ladies gent from miscreants? In the absence of Spenser's lost *English Poet,* the answer is found in Sidney's comments on the relation of the poet's art to nature, a passage already quoted in connection with Bartholomew's Platonic aims (see page 14). Thus it is hardly surprising that Spenser's similes from nature often reflect Bartholomew, who so explicitly states that the phenomenal world exists that "man mai see and know by his inwarde sight intellectual, the divine, celestiall, and godlye things, which are invissibles to this our naturale sight." Clothing moral truth in profitable examples, Spenser employs them to illustrate the feigned exploits of his narrative. In theory the aery encounters are intended to aid the "inwarde sight intellectual." In practice, therefore, Spenser's preoccupation with a familiar province in nature led him to neglect its proper symbolic function in shadowing the world of humanity.

Spenser's undivided attention to the demands of decorum accounts thus far for his inclusion of birds. Similes in the *Faerie Queene* usurp first place in depicting combat or flight, his sympathy frequently for the victim, who corresponds with a helpless female escaping a ravisher. In the minor poems decorum again is in command: the owl and his kind contrast with the singing nightingale, the culver or lark signifies the degeneracy of latter with former happy days.

Occasionally the reader encounters spontaneous allusions to birds as, for instance, when Calepine, now well from a wound (vi. iv. 17):

> cast abrode to wend
> To take the ayre and heare the thrushes song

or when Guyon enters the bedecked "gondelay" of Phaedria (ii. vi. 5):

> Eftsoones her shallow ship away did slide,
> More swift then swallow sheres the liquid skye.

Here the light carefreedom of the owner is enhanced by the comparison. Once, in *Epithalamion,* the poet names five English songbirds together, suggesting by the quality of their song that he is familiar with each. It is the morning of his wedding day (80–82):

> The merry Larke hir mattins sings aloft,
> The thrush replyes, the Mavis descant playes,[23]
> The Ouzell shrills, the Ruddock warbles soft.

[23] Charles Swainson (*Provincial Names and Folk Lore of British Birds,* London, 1885, p. 3) remarks that both mistle thrush and throstle were called mavis. In the above lines "the latter bird is evidently the throstle; the word 'descant' (i.e., the altering the movement of an air by additional notes and ornaments) being an exact description of this bird's song. But, on the other hand, Skelton, in his poem "Phillip Sparow" writes:

'The threstill with her warblynge,
The mavis with her whistell.'

Here the throstle's sweet music is contrasted with the clear, shrill cry of the missel thrush." Todd notes that mavis is usually understood as thrustle

In its momentary abandon, its genuine delight, the passage is like an elaboration of the dawn chorus, with the poet

Joying to heare the birdes sweete harmony.

Nor is there conscious imitation here even of the medieval bird mass, as Van Winkle believes;[24] Spenser's grouping of the five birds is hardly comparable with the formal list, as in Lydgate or Skelton. The "love-learned song" of these birds prompts Spenser's refrain, which, with slight variation, closes each stanza:

That all the woods them answer and theyr eccho ring.

Of this pathetic fallacy in one form or other the poet never tires;[25] a dozen or more examples are noted by Van Winkle. For the refrain of the wedding song Spenser seems to recall Chaucer's delicate rendering of the sentiment in the *Parlement* (201–203):

Ther with a wynd, unnethe it mighte be lesse
Made in the leves grene a softe noyse
Accordant to the foules' song on lofte.

Finally, interesting light is thrown upon Spenser's thinking about birds through his allusions to the cuckoo. As a concluding observation, this subject may serve as a con-

---

or thrush (*Works of Edmund Spenser, Minor Poems,* II, 466): "As the mavis is sometimes mentioned, in our ancient poetry, together with the thrush; I suppose the mavis means the cock-thrush, or song-thrush, the cock being the most distinguished for its tones." Chaucer (*R.R.*) names "thrustils, terins, and mavise," and in the "Tale of Sir Thopas" (1959), "the thrustelcok made eek his lay." See Index.

24 *Works of Edmund Spenser, Minor Poems,* II, 466.

25 Spenser includes also many allusions to bird-singing ("chearfull birds of sundry kynd") as graceful embellishment, usually of an earthly paradise (cf. *F.Q.* i. vii. 3; ii. v. 31; ii. vi. 34; ii. xii. 70, 71; iii. i. 40; iv. x. 45).

venient transition to the discussion of Milton, whose knowledge of the cuckoo more nearly coincides with Chaucer's than with Spenser's.

Two of the *Amoretti* sonnets introduce the cuckoo, and of the first this bird is the theme (19):

The merry cuckow, messenger of Spring,
His trompet shrill hath thrise already sounded,
That warns al lovers wayt upon their king,
Who now is comming forth with garland crouned.
With noyse whereof the quyre of byrds resounded
Their anthemes sweet, devized of Loves prayse,
That all the woods theyr ecchoes back rebounded,
As if they knew the meaning of their layes.
But mongst them all which did Loves honor rayse,
No word was heard of her that most it aught,
But she his precept proudly disobayes,
And doth his ydle message set at nought.
Therefore, O Love, unlesse she turne to thee
Ere cuckow end, let her a rebell be.

In addition to other roles of the cuckoo in folklore, as recounted by Swainson (pp. 109–22), this bird ranks with the swallow as spring's harbinger. But as previously pointed out, in English literary tradition represented in Clanvowe's *The Cuckoo and the Nightingale,* the cuckoo symbolizes ill luck in love and as such opposes the nightingale. If heard first, the cuckoo "warns al lovers," not however to "wayt upon their king," but that the King of Love would not be propitious in that year. Milton adapted this theme from the earlier poem. But Clanvowe's and Milton's "rude bird of Hate" Spenser chose as the perennial symbol of spring, as sign and signal for love's acceptance. His perverse mistress, however, disregarding it, "doth his ydle message set at nought."[26]

It is interesting to observe that later in the sequence Spenser contrasts the notes of cuckoo and mavis, to the disparagement of the bird he has earlier praised (84):

So does the cuckow, when the mavis sings,
Begin his witlesse note apace to clatter.

Writing to order, obviously Spenser does not often give rein to his own sentiments; hence it is difficult to conclude where the cuckoo stands in his affections. Spenser would probably regard this question as impertinent, certainly of secondary importance. In his epic similes he occasionally allows himself to become immersed in the lore of falconry which he suits neatly to his purposes with sometimes unhappy analogy with his protagonists. Chaucer outgrew the romanticism of the *Romaunt,* even the avian conventions of courtly love, to attain the originality of simile in the *Tales;* to the end Spenser remained loyal to poetic law as he knew it.

[26] Spenser records his acceptance in Sonnet LXXIII, the time apparently the spring of 1594. On St. Barnabas' Day, June 11, he was married. The phrase "ere cuckoo end" may refer to June, during which this bird does not actually "end" but changes his tune. Even Matthew Arnold, in *Thyrsis,* mistakenly refers to the "cuckoo's parting cry," as noted by H. J. Massingham, *Poems about Birds* (London, 1923), p. 396.

IV : *Milton*

EVEN AS SPENSER'S ROMANTIC VIEW of caged birds diametrically opposes Chaucer's realistic approach, so Milton scorns Spenser's cuckoo and returns to the tradition of Clanvowe and Chaucer:

O Nightingale, that on yon bloomy spray
  Warbl'st at eeve, when all the Woods are still,
  Thou with fresh hope the Lovers heart dost fill,
  While the jolly hours lead on propitious May,

Thy liquid notes that close the eye of Day,
  First heard before the shallow Cuckoo's bill
  Portend success in love; O if Jove's will
  Have linkt that amorous power to thy soft lay,
Now timely sing, ere the rude Bird of Hate
  Foretell my hopeles doom in som Grove ny:
  As thou from yeer to yeer hast sung too late
For my relief; yet hadst no reason why,
  Whether the Muse, or Love call thee his mate,
  Both them I serve, and of their train am I.

In letter and spirit this sonnet gracefully renders *The Cuckoo and the Nightingale,* by Thomas Clanvowe (1392), which has been described (see pages 28–29). Skeat, who points out the specific parallels, remarks that the medieval piece "was admired by so good a judge of poetry as John Milton, who of course possessed a copy of it in the volume which was so pleasantly called 'The Works of Chaucer.' "[1] The lines of the Middle English poem are as follows:

That it were good to here the nightingale
Rather than the lewde cukkow singe: . . .
A litel hast thou been to longe henne
For here hath been the lewde cukkow,
And songen songes rather than hast thou: . . .
Ye, quod she, and be thou not amayed,
Though thou have herd the cukkow er than me.
For, if I live, it shal amended be
The nexte May, if I be not affrayed: . . .
And I wol singe oon of my songes newe
For love of thee, as loude as I maye crye: . . .

[1] *Chaucerian and Other Pieces: A Supplement to the Poems of Chaucer* (London, Oxford University Press, 1897), p. lxi.

For in this worlde is noon so good servyse
To every wight that gentil is of kinde: . . .

Like Chaucer, who preferred Pliny's nightingale to Ovid's, Milton repeatedly expresses contempt for the cuckoo. His sonnet is a prayer to the nightingale to alter its course of preceding years and, by singing before the cuckoo, "portend success in love."

Disregarding the Ovidian fable of Spenser, Sidney, and the rest, Milton occasionally uses the classical name Philomel, yet still the bird is a symbol of Eros. In Elegy V, addressing "Philomel, hidden in the young leaves," he invokes the nightingale to "begin together, I, in the city, thou, amidst the trees, and let us both together sing the coming of spring." In *Il Penseroso* the poet hopes

Philomel will deign a Song,
In her sweet saddest plight,
Smoothing the rugged brow of night.

The sonnets which have been presented afford unique opportunity to compare the art of Spenser and Milton as both enlist birds in the service of Eros. Of primary interest are the symbolic parts played by nightingale and cuckoo. Aside from their different use of these birds, significantly both poets look upon birds as agents in expressing their own erotic sentiments. Thus, differing in their symbolic use of birds, Spenser and Milton are at one in their poetic aims. Further considerations, however, point to a wide divergence.

In his Third Prolusion, "Against the Scholastic Philosophy," Milton seems to align himself with the new scientific spirit; in so doing he parts company with Spenser.

Nature, not subject to old age, invites the student "to investigate and to observe . . . to plunge the mind into the sacred essences of stones and plants." Study Aristotle, "who indeed has left to us almost all these things, which ought to be learned, written in a scientific manner and with much pains" (XII, p. 171).[2]

Actually, in this century which produced Sir Thomas Browne, Ray, and Willughby, and which, with the founding of the Royal Society, witnessed the collapse of authority and the beginnings of orderly observation, Milton's poetry and prose alike reflect, not Aristotle, but ancient and medieval intermediaries. Milton regards Pliny, Plutarch, and the encyclopedists as the proper repositories of natural history. In satire, where his avian imagery is largely concentrated, Milton's metaphors are reminiscent of William Turner the priest and of the sage and serious Spenser's *Mother Hubberds Tale.* The similes of *Paradise Lost* owe something of their art to the *Faerie Queene,* but whereas for his matter Spenser draws occasionally upon his own observations, as of falconry, Milton depends heavily upon the ancients. And in the story of creation Milton, prompted by Du Bartas, Ralegh, and others, returns to the world of Basil the Great, ancient authority in exegesis. This fact, now to be elaborated, is the keynote to Milton's perspective in so far as it pertains to natural history in general.

Milton's repeated and accurate allusions to Basil, once with an extended quotation, attest the poet's special in-

[2] For the prose works reference is to volume and page in *Works of John Milton,* ed. Frank A. Patterson (18 vols., New York, Columbia University Press, 1931–46).

terest in this great hexaemeron of the fourth century.[3] One of the two notices from the poet's *Commonplace Book* concerns the owl, and it is characteristic in expressing his contemptuous attitude: "Basil compares sophists to owls, for they in matters minute and obscure have eyes or wish to be thought to have them, but in weighty matters of manifest truth and of helpful knowledge are blind; for the owl at night has acute vision but in the daytime sees dimly. Hexam. Homil. 8. 107" (XVIII, p. 138). The passage to which Milton refers is as follows:

Thus those who are zealous of vain knowledge are like the eyes of an owl. For by night indeed its sight is excellent; with the rising sun, however, its sight is obscured: thus indeed the mind of such men is most keen to consider vanity; but for perceiving the true light it waxes dull.

And Hanford has indicated the edition of Basil which Milton used.[4]

Recent criticism has rightly discountenanced efforts to designate the specific authorities upon which Milton depended. With particular reference to the hexaemeral litera-

[3] Citing the Proem of the "Homily on Psalm 1" and accurately quoting the passage, Milton writes: "Basil tells us that poetry was given by God to rouse in human souls the love of virtue" (*Commonplace Book,* XVIII, p. 139); in *Tetrachordon* he calls Basil to witness in support of divorce on grounds other than adultery (IV, p. 211); in *Areopagitica* he recalls Basil's recommendation of "a sportfull poem" by Homer (IV, p. 308). For further references, see *Index,* I.

[4] "Ut illi qui vanae sapientiae student, noctuae oculis sunt similes! Nam ut illius aspectus noctu quidem valet, sole vero illucescente infuscatur: ita istorum mens perspicacissima quidem est ad contemplandam vanitatem, habescit vero ad veram lucem intelligendam." (Migne, *Patrologiae Graecae,* XXIX, p. 182.) Milton used the two-volume edition of Basil, *Opera* (Paris, 1618), according to J. H. Hanford, "The Chronology of Milton's Private Studies," *Publications of the Modern Language Association,* XXXVI (1921), pp. 251–314; see p. 279, note 138.

ture so pervasive in *Paradise Lost,* Williams remarks that "source studies virtually cancel each other";[5] and in later compendiums Williams has found the early fathers copiously cited and excerpted. Yet the text of Basil himself seems never to have been compared with Milton's, though some dozen allusions to, and quotations from, this authority bespeak the poet's direct acquaintance. The following comparisons of Milton's account of creation with the homilies of Basil on this theme are intended to point to the identity of Milton's lore with that originating in the early centuries of the Christian era, and hence it bears directly upon Milton's outlook upon nature. Through precisely what intermediaries the tradition reached him is irrelevant to present purposes. It is important, however, to recognize how fully Milton has forsaken his early Baconian vision. This fact is borne out in considerations to follow.

To describe the working of the Spirit of God Milton twice repeats the timeworn figure of the brooding fowl (*P.L.* i. 20–22):

with mighty wings outspread
Dove-like satst brooding on the vast Abyss
And madst it pregnant.

The account of creation in Book Seven parallels that of Basil (*P.L.* vii. 234 ff.):

but on the watery calm

[5] Arnold Williams, "Commentaries on Genesis as a Basis for Hexaemeral Material in the Literature of the Late Renaissance," *Studies in Philology,* XXXIV (1937), pp. 191–208, especially p. 191. In Pererius and Mercenne the author finds much of Ralegh and Purchas. F. E. Robbins, *The Hexaemeral Literature* (Chicago, University of Chicago Press, 1912), cites several analogues with Milton.

His brooding wings the Spirit of God outspread
And vital virtue infused and vital warmth
Throughout the fluid mass.

From the biblical word *confovebat* Basil had adapted this avian figure:

And thus he imparted to the nature of waters the power of bringing forth young, like a brooding bird imparting a certain vital quality to those which are warmed.[6]

"This passage was much imitated," states Robbins, who names Ralegh and Du Bartas among late followers.[7]

The creation of birds follows that of fish, to which they are closely related (*P.L.* vii. 387–423):

And God said, let the Waters generate
Reptil with Spawn abundant, living Soule:
And let Fowle flie above the Earth, with wings
Displayed on the op'n Firmament of Heav'n.
And God created the great Whales, and each
Soul living, each that crept, which plenteously
The waters generated by their kindes,
And every Bird of wing after his kinde; . . .
Mean while the tepid Caves, and Fens and shoares
Thir Brood as numerous hatch, from the Egg that soon
Bursting with kindly rupture forth disclos'd

[6] "Et ita naturae aquarum vim tribuebat fetificandi, instar incubantis avis, et vitalem quamdam facultatem iis quae foventur impartientis." (Migne, *op. cit.,* p. 43.)

[7] Robbins, *op. cit.,* pp. 48–49. For Du Bartas see George C. Taylor, *Milton's Use of Du Bartas* (Cambridge, Harvard University Press, 1934), pp. 59, 66. The rest of the French account of creation has little or no bearing upon that of Milton. For quotations from Ralegh and Purchas see George W. Whiting, *Milton's Literary Milieu* (Chapel Hill, N.C., University of North Carolina Press, 1939), p. 22. Ralegh's inaccuracies suggest that he was using a commentary rather than the original text of Basil.

Thir callow young, but feather'd soon and fledged
They summ'd thir Penns, and soaring th' air sublime
With clang despis'd the ground, under a cloud
In prospect; . . .[8]

Basil similarly details the kinship of fish and birds:

Why indeed from the waters did he give birth to winged creatures also? Because between flying and swimming creatures there is, as it were, a certain kinship. For just as fish cut through the water, proceeding to distant places by movement of fins, and by movement of the tail now going in a circle, now directing themselves in straight motions, it is possible to see the same thing in flying creatures since in similar manner by means of wings they penetrate the air. Wherefore since the faculty of swimming may be regarded as the same for both, a certain affinity has been bestowed upon them through their generation from the waters.[9]

Milton's eagle and stork, which (424)

[8] Don C. Allen ("Milton and the Creation of Birds," *Modern Language Notes,* LXIII, 1948, pp. 263–64) finds in Plutarch and others discussion of the question, Does the egg precede the hen? But Milton's figure belongs rather to the hexaemeral writers, as the entire context of Book Seven shows. With Milton's soaring birds despising the ground D'Arcy W. Thompson (*Glossary of Greek Birds,* Oxford, 1895, p. 74) compares Vergil, *Geor.* i. 373.

[9] "Cur etiam volatilibus ex aquis ortum dedit? Quia volatilia inter et natatilia quaedam est veluti cognatio. Quemadmodum enim pisces aquam secant, ad ulteriora motu pinnarum progredientes, et caudae mutatione tum circuitiones tum rectos motus sibi ipsis dirigentes: sic et in volatilibus videre est, quandoquidem alis simili modo aerem trajiciunt. Quare cum natandi proprietas in utrisque sit una, una quaedam ipsis affinitas per aquarum generationem collata est." (Migne, *op. cit.,* pp. 167–70.)

For Basil's followers cf. Robbins, *op. cit.,* p. 32, note 3. "Augustine shows that they [birds] are able to fly only in the humid air which is closely akin to water" (*ibid.,* p. 70). He and his successors, Robbins adds, lack the fullness of bird lore found in Basil and Ambrose. Like Du Bartas, Milton follows Basil and the authors influenced by him.

On Cliffs and Cedar tops thir Eyries build

suggest Basil's statement of habitat: "Aliae incolunt montes, ac solitudine delectantur" (p. 171). Milton now proceeds with the stork-crane description (*P.L.* vii. 425–31):

Part loosly wing the Region, part more wise
In common, rang'd in figure wedge their way,
Intelligent of seasons, and set forth
Thir Aierie Caravan high over Sea's
Flying, and over Lands with mutual wing
Easing their flight; so stears the prudent Crane
Her annual Voiage, born on Windes.

This passage is partly explained in Milton's Seventh Prolusion, "In Defence of Knowledge" (XII, p. 253):

How by a very wise and strict custom, do the geese, while flying over the Taurus mountains, lessen the danger of talkativeness by stopping their mouths with pebbles . . . the art of war credits to the cranes the expedient of posting sentries and the triangular order of battle.

Here Milton has been extolling the instinctive wisdom of animals, the subject, he remembers, of a debate in Plutarch, whom he names as his authority.[10] But Svendsen

10 "Which are the Most Crafty, Water or Land Animals," *Plutarch's Morals,* ed. Wm. W. Goodwin, (5 vols., London, n.d.), V, pp. 157–217. Milton cites the reasoning of dogs (*ibid.,* pp. 179–80), of the nightingale, which on Aristotle's authority (iv. 536^b. 18) teaches its young musical rules (p. 189), and of the ibis, which taught man the value of purging the bowels (p. 192). (The blood-letting hippopotamus appears to be lacking in Plutarch.) Then appears the example of geese, which, "while flying over the Taurus mountain, lessen the danger of talkativeness by stopping their mouths with pebbles" (p. 175). Cranes possess a double virtue, Plutarch continues, as they fly in a triangle and, resting at night, hold a stone in their claws to wake them if they allow it to fall. These phenomena are all appropriated by Aelian (ii. 35; iii. 13, 40; v. 29; vi. 59). Plutarch's debate

Gratiam referendam.

Aërio inſignis pietate Ciconia nido
Inueſtes pullos pignora grata fouet,
Taliaq; expectat ſibi munera mutua reddi,
Auxilio hoc quoties mater egebit anus:
Nec pia ſpem ſoboles fallit, ſed feſſa parentum
Corpora fert humeris, preſtat & ore cibos.

Folger Shakespeare Library

". . . bearing them [parents] upon her back
Through th'emptie Aire, when their owne wings they lack;
But also, sparing (this let children note)
Her daintiest food from her own hungry throate."
(Du Bartas, *Devine Weeks,* tr. Sylvester, 1605)

8. Young stork bearing parent. (From Alciati, *Emblematum libellus,* Paris, 1534, p. 9.)

has cited the goose passage in the *Speculum Mundi* (1635), where Swan attributes rightly the pebble device to cranes.[11] In Primaudaye's *The French Academie* he finds (p. 66) that geese fly in triangular order and that the "hindmost do commonly rest their heads upon the foremost, and when the guide is weary of going before, he commeth hindmost, to the end that every one may keep his turne." Thus, Svendsen believes that in the prolusion Milton attributes to the goose a crane tactic and that in the epic he credits the crane with the mutual-aid device of the goose; moreover, Svendsen believes, Milton may have remembered a variant of this latter idea in Bartholomew's statement (on Isidore's authority) that in migration kites bear cuckoos on their shoulders.[12]

Though the passage in question reflects wide reading by Milton, Basil's account of cranes deserves special attention.

---

concerning the virtues of land and water creatures constituted a mine of information for the encyclopedists, especially so in that Plutarch added to Aristotle's account a wealth of anecdote from hearsay; and he freely repeated his natural history as illustration in argument.

[11] Kester Svendsen, "The Prudent Crane," *Notes and Queries,* CLXXXIII (August 1, 1942), pp. 66–67.

[12] Though Robin (*Animal Lore in English Literature,* London, 1932, pp. 63–64) cites Basil, this derives rather from Du Bartas (translated by Josuah Sylvester, 1605), *Devine Weekes,* Week 1, Day 5. The charitable young stork (p. 180):

"Not onely brooding under her warme brest
Their age-chill'd Bodies bed-rid in the nest;
Nor onely bearing them upon her back
Through th' emptie Aire, when their owne wings they lack;
But also, sparing (this let Children note)
Her daintiest food from her own hungry throate, . . ."

Du Bartas repeats the crane devices of setting a watch, holding pebbles, and "in the Clouds forming the forked Y" (p. 182). On Milton's "mutual wing," George Taylor (*op. cit.,* pp. 97–98) notes only the similarity of the above lines on young carrying old, though the one only "perhaps explains" the other. Whiting (*op. cit.,* p. 82) quotes Pliny on cranes in migration.

Milton's phrase "with mutual wing" emphasizes the orderly co-operation of these famous migratory birds. Traditionally two of their habits explain their co-operative reputation: the system of sentries and the aid provided by young for old. Both are elaborated by Basil:

Just so, cranes set up watches by turn; and some sleep but others, encircling, provide entire security for these in their sleep; then, the period of these guards completed, after uttering a cry this crane turns to slumber: the succeeding one renders in his turn the security which it has received. This regular succession you will observe in the flight itself, by learned order.[13]

Basil's phrase "aliae circumeuntes" suggests Milton's "part loosly wing the Region." Then follows the possibly unique statement in Basil in regard to storks: that in flight—and this is Milton's implication in the phrase "with mutual wing"—the young storks laterally support (not carry) the old by means of their wings:

Surrounding the parent suffering from the falling off of its feathers by reason of age, they provide warmth with their own wings and abundantly supply food: indeed even in flight they render it aid, so far as it can be rendered, *gently supporting it by their wings on each side.*[14]

[13] "Ut grues vicissim constituunt excubias; et quidem aliae dormiunt: aliae vero circumeuntes, omnem ipsis securitatem per somnum exhibent; deinde tempore vigiliarum peracto, haec quidem clangore edito ad somnum convertitur: illa vero succedens, securitatem quam accepit, sua vice reddit. Observabis et hunc ordinem in ipso volatu. . . ." (Migne, *op. cit.,* p. 175.)

[14] "Illae genitorem prae senio pennarum defluviis laborantem circumstantes, suismet pennis calefaciunt, suppeditantque abunde alimentum: quin subsidium ei, quoad fieri potest, in ipso volatu praestant, utrinque alis suis leniter sublevantes." (*Ibid.*)

British Museum

"The watchman in his clawes holds fast a stone,
Which letting fall the rest are wak'd anone."
(Chester, *Love's Martyr,* 1601)

9. Sleeping cranes with sentry. (From Harleian MS 4751, fol. 39[a].)

Milton would hardly be troubled by the difficulty of visualizing this charitable act.[15]

The nightingale leads the songbirds which sing until evening (435):

> Nor then the solemn Nightingale
> Ceas'd warbling, but all night tun'd her soft layes.[16]

Basil accurately observes (p. 182): "Quomodo vigil sit luscinia cum avis incubat: quandoquidem *per totam noctem* a cantu non desistit" ("even as the nightingale is awake, when it is incubating, since through the whole night it does not cease its song"). Milton's "swan with arched neck" is the mute swan, not the wild whooper.[17] Basil briefly mentions the swan, its neck sunk in the deep water ("collo in profundam aquam immisso"), in the act of feeding (p. 183). Then (*P.L.* vii. 443–46):

> the crested Cock whose clarion sounds
> The silent hours, and th'other whose gay Traine
> Adorns him, colour'd with the Florid hue

[15] The act Milton so ambiguously described has been otherwise interpreted: "It is a pity that the 'mutual wing' should be a fiction, for the idea that each bird rested its head on the back of the bird before it in the V of their flight is a charming one." (Robinson, *op. cit.*, p. 129.)

[16] Among the poet's seventeen allusions to the nightingale, cf. *P.L.* iii. 37–40:

"Then feed on thoughts, that voluntarie move
Harmonious numbers; as the wakeful Bird
Sings darkling, and in shadiest Covert hid
Tunes her nocturnal Note."

The beauty of Milton's poetry about this bird is unvarying.

[17] "How admirably labour-saving were the foreseeing dispensations of Providence, who on the fifth day created the cock and the swan, all ready domesticated (the wild swan does not arch its neck) before the advent of man on the sixth!" observes H. J. Massingham in *Poems about Birds* (London, 1923), p. 373.

Of Rainbows and Starrie Eyes.[18]

Compare Basil (p. 171): "Superbus est gallus: ornatus et elegantiae amator est pavo" ("Proud is the cock; adorned, a lover of elegance is the peafowl"). Of the cock further (p. 182): "Solem adhuc e loginquo accedentem praenuntians" ("Announcing beforehand the sun as yet approaching from afar"). Milton concludes (446 ff.):

The Waters thus
With Fish replenisht, and the Aire with Fowle,
Ev'ning and Morn solemniz'd the Fift day.

Compare Basil (p. 179): "Habes igitur coelum exornatum, terram decoratam, mare propriis fetibus exuberans, aerem avibus refertum, iisque ipsum pervolantibus" ("You have, accordingly, the sky bedecked, the earth adorned, the sea swelling with its own broods, the air filled with birds, and with them flying"). With his feeling for fertility and exuberant life, Milton would have delighted in this sequence of four synonymous verbs.[19] Basil now turns to the night birds, among them the sophist-like owl which, as it has been seen, appears in the *Commonplace Book.*

In the story of creation, Milton's affinity for the tradition of Basil in idea, in sequence, even in language has been demonstrated. Elsewhere in his verse further reminiscence of this hexaemeron increases the impression of identity in spirit and conception. Basil's full account of the

[18] Taylor (*op. cit.,* p. 98) finds in Sylvester's Du Bartas the cock "crested," the peafowl "with glorious eyes."

[19] "It is a simple and very common feeling, but Milton had it with a force quite exceptional among poets, as if his own teeming brain and soaring temperament were in some intimate way linked with the apparent lavishness of nature in perpetuating the forms of life." (E. M. W. Tillyard, *The Miltonic Setting,* 3d ed., London, 1949, p. 69.)

halcyon is closely analogous to the phrasing in the well-known lines of Milton's ode *On the Morning of Christ's Nativity* (64 ff.):

The Windes with wonder whist,
Smoothly the waters kist,
Whispering new joyes to the milde Ocean,
Who now hath quite forgot to rave,
While Birds of Calm sit brooding on the charmed wave.

Basil's account is as follows:

Almost in mid-winter it hatches its young, at a time when the sea with its many and violent waves is being dashed against the shore. Yet all the winds are lulled to sleep, the ocean surges lie still for seven days during which the halcyon broods.[20]

In his management of epic simile and in the shiplike figure of Satan, Milton's echoes of Spenser are unmistakable.[21] With particular reference to artistry, the backgrounds of the Miltonic simile have been ably studied by James Whaler.[22] For avian imagery the poet may have turned again to ancient authorities. Raphael, reciting to Adam the story of the angelic hosts rallying to battle in

[20] "Circa mediam fere hiemem pullos excludit tum, cum mare multis et violentis ventis ad terram alliditur. Attamen *consopiuntur venti* omnes, quiescunt aequorei fluctus per septem dies, quibus halcyon avis incubat." (Migne, *op. cit.*, p. 178.) Italics supplied. In Pliny "the sea is calm and navigable"; in Sir Thomas Browne "the windes do cease." (Whiting, *op. cit.*, p. 86.)

[21] Cf. present study, pp. 71–72. With Spenser's soaring dragon, depicted in falconry terms (*F.Q.* i. 11), Upton compares *P.L.* i. 225; ii. 927–30; iii. 741; and iv. 568 (*Works of Edmund Spenser*, variorum ed., 9 vols., Baltimore, Johns Hopkins Press, 1932–49, I, pp. 298–99).

[22] "The Miltonic Simile," *Publications of the Modern Language Association*, XLVI (1931), pp. 1034–74; and "Animal Simile in 'Paradise Lost,'" *Publications of the Modern Language Association*, XLVII (1932), pp. 534–53.

heaven, compares them with the birds which trooped to Adam to receive their names (*P.L.* vi. 73–76):

as when the total kind
Of Birds in orderly array on wing
Came summoned over *Eden* to receive
Thir names of thee.

This simile, which is, as Whaler remarks, "the only one perfectly mated to Adam's comprehension," suggests a like immensity of conception described by Isidore; Basil's last homily comes short of this event. Isidore writes:

Adam first gave names to all animals, calling each according to its inherent disposition and according to the work for which nature intended it to be fitted. To each of the animals peoples have given names from their own tongue. . . . For no one can discover how many kinds of birds there are.[23]

The fine comparison of Satan to the vulture flying toward Indian streams (*P.L.* iii. 431 ff.) has its geographical origin in Ortelius' map, as Whiting has shown.[24] A second and more descriptive vulture simile is of ancient origin (*P.L.* x. 273–80):

As when a flock
Of ravenous Fowl, though many a League remote,
Against the day of Battel, to a Field,
Where Armies lie encampt, come flying, lur'd
With sent of living Carcasses design'd

[23] "Omnibus animalibus Adam primum vocabula indidit, appellans unicuique nomen ex praesenti institutione, juxta conditionem naturae cui serviret. Gentes autem unicuique animalium ex propria lingua dederunt vocabula. . . . Nam volucrum quot genera sint, invenire quisquam non potest." (Migne, *op. cit.*, pp. 423–24, 459.)

[24] *Op. cit.*, pp. 117–18.

For death, the following day, in bloodie fight.
So sented the grim Feature, and upturn'd
His Nostril wide into the murkie Air, . . .

For this simile two early vulture passages are illustrative. The first is from Basil:

Who foretells to vultures the death of men at a time when they wage mutual war upon themselves? You can see innumerable *flocks* of vultures following *armies,* and divining the outcome from the preparations of arms.[25]

Isidore now supplies the repeated idea of "sent," referring explicitly to sight, not to odor:

Vultures also, like eagles, sight ["sentiunt"] corpses even across seas: flying higher indeed they descry from aloft the numbers hidden by the gloom of mountains.[26]

In reversing the traditional belief, Milton accidentally hits upon the general agreement of modern science with regard to this vexing problem.

Reverently Milton approached the sequence of creation as recounted in the hexaemera; a different spirit now animates his prose. There his bird metaphors are invariably contemptuous, as, intent upon vilifying his opponent, he recalls the traditionally obscene, the ignorant, the ranting characteristics of birds. For subject matter the hexaemeral writers are again apropos. In *Tetrachordon* the ostrich is

[25] "Quis praenuntiat vulturibus hominum mortem tum, cum sibi invicem inferunt bellum? Videas enim innumeros *greges* vulturum *exercitus* sequentes, et ex armorum apparatu *exitum conjectantes.*" (Migne, *op. cit.,* p. 182.) Italics supplied.

[26] "Vultures autem, sicut et aquilae, etiam ultra maria cadavera sentiunt; altius quippe volantes multa quae montium obscuritate celantur ex alto illae conspiciunt" (Migne, *op. cit.,* p. 460.) *Cf.* Aelian (ii. 46), "Vultures carnis humanae appetentes."

Bodleian Library

"The Iron-eating Estridge."
(Drayton, *Noahs Flood,* 1630)

10. Ostriches with horseshoes. (From Johann von Cube, *Hortus Sanitatis,* Mainz, 1491, fol. 330^{a}.)

apparently credited also with a raven attribute (IV, pp. 87–88):

The common Expositers . . . give us in such a manner, as they who leav their own mature positions like the eggs of an Ostrich in the dust; I do but lay them in the sun; their own pregnancies hatch the truth; and I am taxt of novelties and strange producements, while they, like that inconsiderat bird, know not that these are their own naturall breed.

Compare Isidore on the ostrich:

It neglects to warm its eggs, which, cast aside only, are hatched in the warmth of dust.

And on the raven:

They say that this bird does not freely provide food for its fledglings until it recognizes a blackness like its own hue in their feathers. After it has perceived their hideous plumes, more abundantly it feeds them wholly approved. This bird first seeks the eye in corpses.[27]

This last idea Milton alludes to in *Animadversions* (III, pt. 1, p. 172): Bishops are "ravens . . . that would peck out the eyes of all knowing Christians" (he has just termed them "vultures gorging themselves on the bait of church livings").

In the sonnet on the reception of *Tetrachordon* Milton scornfully terms his critics owls and cuckoos. Basil's comparison of owls and sophists is apropos the first, and the nightingale sonnet shows the poet's contempt for the

[27] "Ova sua fovere negligit, sed projecta tantummodo, fotu pulveris animantur. . . . Fertur haec avis, quod editis pullis escam plene non praebeat, priusquam in eis per pennarum nigredinem similitudinem proprii coloris agnoscat. Postquam vero eos tetros plumis aspexerit, in toto agnitos abundantius pascit. Hic prior in cadaveribus oculum petit." (*Ibid.*, pp. 461, 465.)

Milton here remembers Job 39:14–16: the ostrich "leaveth her eggs in the earth, and warmeth them in dust. And forgetteth that the foot may crush them, or that the wild beast may break them. She was hardened against her young ones as though they were not hers"; and Lamentations 4:3: "cruel like the ostriches in the wilderness." Neckam (p. 101) identifies the bird with the hypocrite and emphasizes its neglect of the eggs, warmed by sight alone. Contradictorily, Aelian (xiv. 7) praises the bird's great solicitude for its young.

Gula.

CVRCVLIONE *gruis tumida vir pingitur aluo,*
Qui Laron, aut manibus gestat Onocrotalum.
Talis forma fuit Dionysî, & talis Apicî,
Et gula quos celebres deliciosa facit.

University of Texas Library

"And by his side rode loathsome Gluttony, . . .
His belly was upblowne with luxury, . . .
And like a crane his necke was long and fyne,
With which he swallowed up excessive feast. . . ."
(Spenser, *Faerie Queene,* 1590)

11. Gluttony with symbolic birds. (From Alciati, *Omnia emblemata,* Rome, 1584, p. 201.)

cuckoo. In the First Defence (VII, p. 343) madness has turned Salmasius into a cuckoo, singing "the same ill-omened song over and over again," and later (345–46) he is "a raving, distracted cuckoo." Finally, in *Eikonoclastes* (V, p. 224) the use of set forms of prayer is attributed to constancy, "as if it were Constancie in the Cuckoo to be alwaies in the same Liturgy."

This manner of finding avian analogues for his enemies suggests the Renaissance satire of the priest-naturalist William Turner. In his *Spirituall Physik* (1555) Turner castigates the covetous man in terms of the kite (85r):

As for the ravenous ryche stertuppes, me thynke it were best that ye folowed the byrdes, whych when they sawe the vayne glorious crow as Esop telleth, braggyng her selfe of her false nobilitie, toke eche one theyr owne fethers from her, and sent her to the donghyll agayne, from whence she came.

This is precisely the savage spirit in which Milton turns to Aesop for abuse of Morus (*Pro Se Defensio,* IX, pp. 201–203):

I cannot describe the marvellous variety of borrowed plumes and colours, with which he is suddenly bedecked: you would be inclined to think him some bird of phoenix-wing. . . . You would have declared that men had plucked the birds of Aristophanes; but, if I am not mistaken, they must have been birds of ill-omen: when he is stripped, he will find that he is not now acting a play, but showing the application of one of Aesop's fables in his own person: for when I shall make it appear, More, that these plumes are not your own . . . it is not to be doubted, that the flight of birds before decoyed by you, having at last discovered who you are, will enter an action against you for the embezzlement of their plumes; and that, when each has taken his own, you will be left in the end no phoenix indeed, but a fowl-feeding hoopoe with not a single plume, and barely a breech.

In Milton's figure Morus begins as Horace's daw (chough) becomes a phoenix and finally, shorn of his stolen plumes, a hoopoe, a proverbially filthy bird.[28] Even the victimized brilliant ones have become the dull-plumaged birds of ill omen. Throughout, the reminiscence of Turner is inescapable.

Scattered general allusions to birds seem instinctively contemptuous. In the well-known passage from *Areopagitica* the majestic eagle traditionally "nuing her youth" is set over against "the noise of timorous and flocking birds, with those also that love the twilight, . . . in their envious gabble." At Cambridge, he remarks in the Seventh Prolusion (XII, p. 277), "Not men, but just finches indeed feed on thistles and thorns." He castigates Hall in terms of plucking a gull (*Apol.*, III, p. 310): "[I am] already weary of pluming and footing this Seagull, so open he lies to strokes." Professor Banks reports that 47 per cent of Milton's animal imagery concerns birds and that of this more than half involves snaring, though quadrupeds are apparently intended at times. "Furthermore, in sympathy for the snared bird, so evident in Shakespeare, Milton is almost wholly lacking."[29] To Shakespeare can be added Spenser. The sneer, "a few grains of corn to intice the silly fowl to enter the nest" (*Brief Notes*, VI, p. 157) is more charac-

[28] Cf. Pliny, x. 29, "avis obscoena pastu." The accumulated excrement in the nest of the incubating hoopoe accounts for its reputation for obscenity.
[29] Theodore H. Banks, *Milton's Imagery* (New York, 1950), p. 154.

teristic than the metaphor picturing the lady's plight in *Comus* (565–66):

And O poor hapless Nightingale thought I,
How sweet thou sings't, how neer the deadly snare!

But the danger of generalizing is apparent as one recalls other such lyric passages about birds, and these are numerous. *Comus* includes the striking image depicting contemplation (374 ff.):

Wisdoms self
Oft seeks to sweet retired Solitude,
Where with her best nurse Contemplation
She plumes her feathers, and lets grow her wings
That in the various bustle of resort
Were all too ruffl'd, and sometimes impair'd.

The morning skylark, like the nightingale—both usually hackneyed—always receives new impress from Milton's pen. Compare *Paradise Regained* (ii. 279–82):

Thus wore out the night, and now the Herald Lark
Left his ground-nest, high towring to descry
The morns approach, and greet her with his Song:
As lightly from his grassy Couch up rose
Our Saviour.

Such passages are inconspicuous only in comparison to the number of those in the prose. Thus, for Milton the bird world was largely useful in providing symbols of despicable human attributes. Neither Spenser nor Milton shared appreciably Chaucer's wholehearted delight in birds, their songs, their absurdities of mood and appearance. Milton differed from Spenser in his early sympathy for the new scientific outlook. The foregoing survey within the narrow area of bird lore supports the broader thesis that, in the words of Bush, Milton "had not abjured his basic belief that there is a gulf between the knowledge of external nature and the knowledge of God and the supreme ends of life."[30] Milton's poetry of birds is always impressive; it gives little hint, however, of any genuine interest in their world.

[30] Douglas Bush, *Science and English Poetry* (London, Oxford University Press, 1950), p. 46.

V : *Drayton*

The preceding chapters have made clear the extent to which poetry clung to the medieval approach in natural history. Chaucer's objective view of nature, his refusal to sentimentalize, allied him actually more nearly with the seventeenth century than with the Elizabethans. But in theory and practice Spenser and Milton depended almost exclusively upon the symbolic encyclopedias.

With Michael Drayton it is a different story. The poetry to be dealt with in the present chapter covers roughly the first quarter of the seventeenth century, later distinguished by the founding of the Royal Society and, in ornithology, by the publication of the work of Willughby and Ray (*Ornithologia,* 1676). Drayton began in the medieval manner illustrated in the prose tracts of Turner. Yet gradually as he became interested in birds, his verse began to reflect both this new, objective observation and also written authority. These united with Drayton's consummate skill in description to produce a new poetry about birds. The reader is aware of the poet's genuine enthusiasm, which does not, however, intrude upon an objective manner suggestive of the scientific attitude. By and large, Drayton thus recapitulates the poetry of birds which has been reviewed in the preceding chapters. In other words, his verse reflects his evolution from the symbolic milieu to that represented by the scientific Turner, whose work Drayton recognized as authoritative. These facts, then, made it inevitable that chronology should be disregarded and that not Milton but Drayton should conclude the present study.

Aside from the many scattered allusions to birds throughout Drayton's verse, four poems contain extensive lists. Each denotes a special interest in bird life, yet each bears the impress of supplementary study of current authority.[1] These are, in the order of their composition: *The Owle* (1603), *The Man in the Moone* (1606), *Polyolbion,* Song XIII (1612) and Song XXV (1622), and *Noahs*

[1] For information about plants Drayton consulted Dodoens and Gerard; see Thomas P. Harrison, "Drayton's Herbals," *University of Texas Studies in English,* XXIII (1943), pp. 15–25.

Flood (1630). The significance of his descriptive passages lies not in their exactness when compared with modern ornithological distinctions but in the fact that half a century before Ray and Willughby the poet Drayton is making keen observations of birds for their own sake. This approach, it will appear, reflects the poet's gradual emergence from the medievalism of *The Owle.*

Drayton's *The Owle,* 1304 lines in heroic couplets, is interesting chiefly by contrast with the later poems. Using the conventions of dream, bird fable, and debate from Chaucer's *The Parlement of Foules,* the Scottish *Buke of the Howlat,* and Spenser's *Mother Hubberds Tale,* the poet attacks various political and social evils: sale of bishoprics, place-hunting and flattery, oppression of the poor, marital infidelity, and the like.[2] More pronounced in Drayton's later work, the influence of Chaucer's prototype, Alanus' *De planctu naturae,* is apparent here in its emphasis upon the symbolism of birds presented catalogue fashion. Inevitably Pliny serves also as an important source of morality. The initial lines strike the poem's tone: the swallow teaches cleanliness, and the kite gives lessons in steering and the crane in ballasting ships and marching in war. But in this wholesale castigation of vice Drayton introduces also less conventional folklore and fable. The kite, for example (390 ff.), assumes the additional role of the Aesopian crow which beautifies himself with feathers of other birds, a fable strikingly like Milton's (see pages 105–106). Similarly, the redbreast, which initially symbolizes charity (87),

[2] See *The Works of Michael Drayton,* ed. J. W. Hebel (London, Oxford University Press, 1931–41), Introduction and notes by Tillotson and Newdigate, V, pp. 174–81.

Covering with Mosse the deads unclosed eye,

later in the poem (719 ff.) usurps the part of his proverbial mate, the wren, as he hides in the plumage of the eagle[3] and, borne thus to new heights, spies upon

His Soveraignes Counsailes, and Joves Secrets heares.

Such a manner of introducing birds as individual persons or as human types—the kestrel a rack-renting landlord, the cormorant a monopolist, the sparrow a luxurious courtier—belongs to an age prior to Drayton's. As in Milton, significant analogy is presented in the work of the earlier Turner, whose *Spirituall Physik* (1555) undertook to satirize abuses in both court and church by representing, like Drayton, various delinquents in the accepted characters of animals, chiefly birds. Here there is practically no hint of the observations resulting in Turner's treatise on birds; similarly *The Owle* evinces as little promise of the poet's later work. In *The Man in the Moone* and, even more clearly, in *Polyolbion* the manner of Turner in *Spirituall Physik* gives way to that found in the *History of Birds*. The significant point here, however, is that Drayton's *The Owle,* with its blending of symbolism, fable, and folklore, belongs wholly to the past. His next poem introducing birds sounds a new note.

The Man in the Moone (1606) is a severely revised and condensed *Endimion and Phoebe* (1595), the poet now returning to the world of classic myth. Of the revision Dray-

3 For lore of robin and wren, cf. Charles Swainson, *Provincial Names and Folk Lore of British Birds* (London, 1885), pp. 17–18 and 36, respectively. For names as for other historical and local lore, see Alfred Newton, *A Dictionary of Birds* (London, 1893–96).

ton's editors remark: "The most effective passage is the strictly irrelevant description of the sea and the waterfowl, as portrayed on Phoebe's mantle: an unexpected piece of medievalism that gives Drayton an opportunity for his favorite *catalogue raisonné.* (It also reveals for the first time that close first-hand observation of birds which may be seen more clearly in Polyolbion.)"[4] But this passage is medieval only in that it imitates the manner of Alanus, whose birds are depicted in the mantle of Nature. (In *The Parlement of Foules* Chaucer's birds are grouped around her.) This significant interpolation, it now appears, stands midway between the sheer medievalism of *The Owle* and the Renaissance *Polyolbion.*

Unlike the traditionally symbolic birds of Alanus, Drayton's list comprises twelve aquatic birds, the same group he had noted in Sylvester's familiar translation of Du Bartas.[5] To Drayton's encyclopedic Muse, Du Bartas was an inevitable favorite; as a poet of birds the Frenchman would be of special interest. Singling out this thread of influence, comparison of the two passages at hand shows Drayton enlarging upon and giving life to Sylvester's dead canvas. Here for the first time his eyes are upon the individual habits of birds; with the names from Du Bartas, observation from life has begun to replace the catalogue. In *Devine Weekes* Sylvester writes (Week 1, Day 5, p. 179):

[4] *The Works of Michael Drayton,* V, p. 190.

[5] Josuah Sylvester, *Bartas His Devine Weeks and Workes* (1605), (parts were issued in 1592, 1595, and 1598). The general similarity is noted by Drayton's editors (*The Works of Michael Drayton,* V, p. 191). First observed in *Endimion and Phoebe* (cf. *ibid.,* V, pp. 19 ff.), the influence of Du Bartas is pervasive in Drayton's poetry; twice he alludes directly to *Les Sepmaines* and its English translation (cf. *ibid.,* III, pp. 230, 358).

But (gentle Muse) tell me what Fowles are those
That but even now from flaggie Fennes arose?
'Tis the hungry Hearn, the greedy Cormorant,
The Coote and Curlew, which the Moores doo haunt,
The nimble Teale, the Mallard strong in flight,
The Di-Dapper, the Plouer and the Snight:[6]
The siluer Swanne, that dying singeth best,
And the Kings-Fisher, which so builds her nest
By the Sea-side in midst of Winter Season. . . .
So long as, there her quiet Couch she keepes
Sicilian Sea exceeding calmely sleepes. . . .

This passage is closely similar to the following from Drayton's *The Man in the Moone* (183–206):

The greedie *Sea-maw* fishing for the fry,
The hungry *Shell-fowle,* from whose rape doth flye
Th' unnumbred sholes, the *Mallard* there did feed.
The *Teale* and *Morecoot* raking in the Weed.
And in a Creeke where waters least did stirre,
Set from the rest the nimble *Divedopper,*
That comes and goes so quickly and so oft
As seemes at once both under and aloft:
The jealous *Swan,* there swimming in his pride,
With his arch'd brest the Waters did divide,
His saily wings him forward strongly pushing,
Against the billowes with such furie rushing,
As from the same, a fome so white arose,

[6] These three birds do not appear in the French original. Cf. *Upon the Death of Henry Raynsford* (*The Works of Michael Drayton,* III, p. 30):
"And *Sylvester* who from the *French* more weake
Made *Bartas* of his sixe days labour speake
In naturall *English,* who, had he there stayd,
He had done well, and never had bewraid,
His owne invention, to have bin so poore
Who still wrote lesse, in striving to write more."

As seem'd to mocke the brest that them oppose:
And here and there the wandring eye to feed,
Oft scattered tufts of Bul-rushes and Reed,
Segges, long-leav'd Willow, on whose bending spray,
The pide *Kings-fisher,* having got his prey,
Sate with the small breath of the water shaken,
Till he devour'd the Fish that he had taken.
The long-neck'd *Herne,* there watching by the brimme,
And in a Gutter neere againe to him
The bidling *Snite,* the *Plover* on the Moore,
The *Curlew,* scratching in the Oose and Ore: . . .

Except for the cormorant, to appear in *Polyolbion,* and the first two birds in Drayton (the "sea-maw" and the sheldrake) the two lists correspond. The name *morecoot* Drayton possibly confuses with moor hen or water hen, the common gallinule. But where Sylvester only names the "didapper"[7] (grebe) Drayton presents an admirable sketch of its well-known habit. In place of Du Bartas' conventional swan "that dying singeth best" and his timeworn kingfisher nesting upon the calm sea, Drayton depicts the beautiful mute swan which he knew on the Thames, then, in four lines, the kingfisher on a willow as it prepares to swallow its prey. Here are sketches from life, not dried specimens from the lore of Pliny and the medievalists. Drayton loses interest in his original as Du Bartas wanders on describing the mysterious "langa" that feeds on whale's heart, the "cucuio" (not a bird, but a firefly) and the exotic "mamuques," or birds of paradise. The final figures on Cynthia's mantle are those of a fowler and a fisherman

[7] The text of 1606 reads, like Sylvester, "didopper," not "divedopper," as in the text of 1619.

(207–20), mention of which also closes the account of Lincolnshire birds in *Polyolbion,* Song XXV (139–40):

The toyling *Fisher* here is towing of his Net:[8]
The *Fowler* is imployd his lymed twigs to set.

Before proceeding to the waterfowl of the Lincolnshire fens, a brief digression is in order concerning an earlier passage in the first part of *Polyolbion* (1612). Drayton's praise of the Warwickshire songbirds (Song XIII, 41–86) has long been admired. "This magnificent passage seems to express the music of the birds in their chorus at dawn in spring. No literary source for his account of the birds has come to light. Drayton is writing from his own knowledge of the birds in the Warwickshire Woodland."[9] Still, in this panegyric, as in the lines already considered, Du Bartas again anticipated Drayton. Though here Drayton is more independent, Sylvester's lines are not insignificant.

The English passage, comprising fourteen species, begins with eloquent delineation of the three famous songbirds—throstle (mavis), merle (blackbird), and nightingale; the others are more briefly listed (Song XIII, 72–80):

To *Philomell* the next, the Linet we prefer;
And by that warbling bird, the Wood-Larke place we then,
The Red-sparrow, the Nope, the Red-breast, and the Wren,
The Yellow-pate: which though she hurt the blooming tree,
Yet scarce hath any bird a finer pype than shee.
And of these chaunting Fowles, the Goldfinch not behind,

[8] This figure possibly derives from Marlowe's *Hero and Leander* (iv. 84 ff.), ultimately from Theocritus' *Idyl* 1.

[9] *The Works of Michael Drayton,* V, p. 237.

That hath so many sorts descending from her kind.
The Tydie for her notes as delicate as they,
The laughing Hecco, then the counterfetting Jay.

Here Drayton is engaged only in naming and praising English songbirds, there being no description of appearance or habit, as so abundantly of the water birds. Of these names only two have offered difficulty: the "nope," a contraction of article and substantive in "an alp" and usually identified with the bullfinch (see Chapter II, "Chaucer," page 33) and "tydie," probably the great tit.[10]

The corresponding passage of Du Bartas is less distinctive and equally undescriptive (Week 1, Day 5, pp. 175–77):

The sent-strong Swallow . . . the prettie *Larke*
The Spinck, the Linote, and the Gold-Finch. . . .
But all this's nothing to the *Nightingale*. . . .
The *Colchian* Pheasant, and the Partridge rare,
The lustful Sparrow, and the fruitfull Stare,
The chattering Pye, the chastest Turtle Dove,
The grizell Quoist,[11] the Thrush that Grapes doth love,

[10] Alfred Newton and A. Smythe Palmer (*Notes and Queries,* 5th Ser., VII, 1877, pp. 12–13) have identified "red-sparrow," "nope," "yellow pate," "tydie," and "hecco" (see Index). As for "tidy," F. P. Wilson (*Philological Quarterly,* XVII, 1938, pp. 216–18) contradicts Urban T. Holmes's argument (*Philological Quarterly,* XVI, 1937, pp. 65–67) for the little owl by showing that *tidie* (*tiddy*) and *tidley* are applied in Warwickshire and Somersetshire to the golden-crested wren and the blue tit, respectively. Recently it has been argued that *tydie* and *tidif* (as in Chaucer) were applied to the great tit, whereas Drayton's "Mistress Titmouse, a neat merrie Dame" properly describes the blue tit; see Charlotte Macdonald, in *Review of English Studies,* XXI (1945), pp. 127–33.

[11] French "la palombe grisarde," English "queest," "cushat," or "ring dove."

The little Gnat-snap, worthy Princes Boords,
And the greene Parrot, fainer of our words.

Sylvester's only serious lapse is the substitution of the starling ("stare") for Du Bartas' "tourt" (throstle), included among Drayton's songbirds. If Drayton consulted Sylvester, the goldfinch,

That hath so many sorts descending from her kind,

includes "spinck" (chaffinch) and "linote" (linnet). Drayton's line uniquely reflects his awareness of current scientific classification, for the finches (*Fringillidae*) are the largest of avian families. Finally, in the last line it looks as if Drayton has substituted "the counterfetting Jay" for Du Bartas' exotic parrot.

Whatever the origins of Drayton's inventory of his native Warwickshire songbirds, he manifests a real delight in their music. But subsequent passages show that his major interest lies with water birds. Larger, their colors and habits might be more easily observed, and in early days their vast numbers as well as their value as food brought them more forcibly to the attention.

So far as birds are concerned, the proper sequel to the group in *The Man in the Moone* is found not in Warwickshire but in the fens of Lincolnshire. In his long and tedious labors by which the English counties—their geography, natural history, local legends, and so forth—are chronicled in Alexandrines, Drayton must have looked forward with delight to Lincolnshire (Song XXV) with its wealth of waterfowl. Observation now fully enters into Drayton's descriptions, supplemented as they are by recourse to specific authority: Turner (1544), Caius (1570), Belon

(1555), and Gesner (1555).[12] Briefly he returns to Du Bartas, whose work perhaps directed him to Belon;[13] and of course throughout *Polyolbion* is reflected the guiding hand of Camden, whose *Britannia* appeared first in 1586 and was reprinted often in succeeding years. Song XXV belongs to the second installment of *Polyolbion,* issued in 1622. The fourteen years since *The Man in the Moone* had extended Drayton's knowledge of birds and matured his art in depicting them.

Water birds now reappear in the boasts of Holland, a district of Lincolnshire. Of a total of twenty-six birds (Song XXV, 52–138) nine had been named by Du Bartas.[14] Commencing with mallard and teal, "the Falconers onely sport," Drayton individualizes the French "cane au large bec, qui sifle de son aile"[15] (omitted in Sylvester) by naming wigeon and goldeneye, the two whistlers, though only the latter bird "whistles within its wing." The new birds, seventeen in all,[16] are introduced, not catalogue fashion, but usually with careful delineation either of distinctive habits, as in *The Man in the Moone,* or, even more frequently, of coloration. Examples now illustrate the manner in which ornithology is popularized in English verse.

[12] For titles, see pp. 22, 25.

[13] Cf. Urban T. Holmes and Others (eds.), *Works of . . . Du Bartas* (Chapel Hill, N.C., University of North Carolina Press, 1935–40), II. The notes contain full record of corresponding birds described by Belon.

[14] Namely, heron, cormorant, coot, curlew, teal, mallard, grebe ("dobchick"), snipe, and swan.

[15] Belon (*Histoire de la Nature des Oyseaux,* Paris, 1555, p. 160) alludes to the ducks which "font bruit de leurs aelles en volant."

[16] Namely, gallinule ("water-hen"), goosander, wigeon, goldeneye, pochard ("smeath"), water ouzel ("water-woosel"), puffin, crane, water rail ("bidcock"), pool snipe ("redshanke"), bittern, goose, barnacle, gull ("sea-meaw" and "gull"), oystercatcher ("sea-pye"), and osprey. (Identifications from Newton, *op. cit.*)

With fair accuracy Drayton describes the "gossander," properly goosander or merganser,

His head as *Ebon* blacke, the rest as white as Snow.

The coot he now distinguishes from the water hen or moor hen, the gallinule (the "morecoot" of *The Man in the Moone*):

The *Coot,* bald, else cleane black, that whiteness it
doth beare
Upon the forehead star'd, the *Water-Hen* doth weare
Upon her little tayle, in one small feather set.

The lines on the bittern manifest a true knowledge of its lore and name:

. . . in some small Reedy bed, . . .
The Buzzing Bitter sits, which through his hollow Bill,
A sudden bellowing sends, which many times doth fill
The neighboring *Marsh* with noyse, as though a Bull did roare.

Traditionally the bittern's loud booming was said to be caused by the bird's inserting its bill into either the water (see Chapter II, "Chaucer," page 44) or a reed; Drayton implicitly denies both notions. In comparing the sound with a bull's roar, he remembers the classical generic name for the bittern, *Botaurus.* According to Belon (p. 193): "Mettant son bec en l'eau, il fait un si gros son, qu'il n'y a beuf qui peust crier si haut . . . dont il a gaigné son nom Latin Taurus." Again Drayton's lines reflect books as well as observation.

The puffin, writes Drayton in traditional vein,

Nice pallats hardly judge, if it be flesh or fish.

Or, as Nashe picturesquely terms this sea bird, "half fish, halfe flesh, a John Indifferent, and an ambodexter betwixt either."[17] Gesner writes skeptically of the "Puffinus Anglorum": "Also it is eaten in Lent because in a measure it seems related to the fishes, in that it is cold-blooded. . . . The English call it *puffin,* which nature made a bird . . . a bird not-a-bird or also a fish."[18] This information was doubtless furnished Gesner by the English Caius, who in his later published letter to the Swiss naturalist writes: "It is used as fish among us during the solemn fast of Lent: being in substance and looke not unlike a Seal."[19] Later, writing of Yorkshire's East Riding (Song XXVIII, 499–506), Drayton repeats a curious story of the habits of the puffin ("mullet") and its frequent companion, the auk:

The *Mullet,* and the *Auke,* (my Fowlers there doe finde)
Of all great *Britain* brood, Birds of the strangest kind,
That building in the Rocks, being taken with the hand,
And cast beyond the Cliffe, that poynteth to the land,
Fall instantly to ground, as though it were a stone,
But put out to the Sea, they instantly are gone,
And flye a league or two before they doe returne,
As onely by that ayre, they on their wings were borne.

This is a slight misconstruction of the simple fact that these birds can take wing more easily from the edge of a cliff or

[17] *Lenten Stuffe,* cited by E. Phipson, *The Animal-Lore of Shakespeare's Time* (London, 1883), p. 293.

[18] "Editur etiam quadragesimae tempore, quod videatur quoddamodo piscibus affinis, cum sanguinem frigidiorem habeat. . . . Angli puffinum, quem avem natura fecit, . . . avem non avem vel autem piscem faciunt." (Gesner, *De avium natura,* Zurich, 1555, p. 110.)

[19] "In piscis usu apud nos est in solenni ieiunio per quadragesimam: carne et gustu, Phocae marinae haud dissimilis." (A. H. Evans, ed., *Turner on Birds,* London, Cambridge University Press, 1903, pp. 204–205.)

from the water. Though Camden does not mention these cliff dwellers, an addition to the 1695 translation of *Britannia* accurately describes the habits of four sea birds, among which are the puffin and the razor-billed auk: "These sorts cannot raise themselves upon the wing from the land, but if at any distance from the cliffs, wadle . . . to some precipice, and thence cast themselves off, and take wing: but from the water they will raise to any height."[20] Possibly Drayton recalls Caius' ambiguous observation that the puffin "does not trust to its wings save in sight of the sea."[21]

In considerations touching *The Man in the Moone* it has been indicated that, instead of Du Bartas' singing swan, Drayton sketches an admirable scene of the semidomesticated swan as it breasts the river current. Returning to Song XXV, one encounters an interesting passage in which the poet now distinguishes the wild whooping swan (*Cygnus musicus* or *ferus*) from this mute bird (*Cygnus olor* or *mansuetus*) (85–90):

Here in my vaster Pooles, as white as Snow or Milke,
(In water blacke as *Stix*) swimmes the wild Swanne, the Ilke,
Of *Hollanders* so tearm'd, no niggard of his breath,
(As Poets say of Swannes, which onely sing in death)
But oft as other Birds, is heard his tunnes to roat,
Which like a Trumpet comes, from his long arched throat.

Thus again Drayton rejects the traditional fable. Not unlikely, he had observed the wild swan in the Lincolnshire fens, a wintering ground for these beautiful and distinc-

20 "Additions to Pembrokeshire," *Britannia,* tr. E. Gibson (London, 1695), p. 639.

21 Evans, *op. cit.,* pp. 206–207: "Alis non confidit nisi conspecto mari."

tive birds from northern Europe. Giraldus had distinguished the two birds, in the twelfth century (see pages 20–21). Even Belon, a pioneer in anatomy, describes only the mute swan with its mythology; Gesner comments upon the etymology of the term *elk*.[22] It remained for the Italian Aldrovandi (1600) to describe the peculiar vocal organs of the whooper. But curiously enough he applied the results of his dissection as proof, not that the wild swan alone trumpets sonorously in flight, but that the fable of the dying swan, usually identified with the mute species, is scientifically valid. This vulgar error is detailed by Sir Thomas Browne later in the century (1646).[23]

But Drayton does not always reject traditional, untried beliefs. Twice he reverts to the older manner. With respectful deference Holland repeats the two current theories about the hatching of barnacle geese (113–14):

> . . . wheresoere they breed
> On Trees, or rotten Ships, yet to my Fennes for feed . . .

The later account of the Isle of Man (Song XXVII, 303–11) develops the first belief. With their roots in water, trees

> send from their stocky bough
> A soft and sappy Gum, from which those Tree-geese grow,
> Call'd *Barnacles* by us, which like a Jelly first
> To the beholder seeme, then by the fluxure nurst,
> Still great and greater thrive, until you well may see

22 Belon, *op. cit.*, pp. 151–52; Gesner, *op. cit.*, pp. 358–59, mentions the cognate forms *alb, elbs, elps,* and *albsch* (cf. Mod. Ger. *Elbschwan*).

23 Of the peculiar vocal organ a marginal note states: "The figuration to be found in Elks, and not in common swans," *Pseudodoxia Epidemica,* Bk. III, Chap. 27. (*Works of Sir Thomas Browne,* ed. Geoffrey Keynes, London, 1928, II, p. 291.)

University of Texas Library

"[Trees] send from their stocky bough
A soft and sappy Gum, from which those Tree-geese grow,
Call'd *Barnacles* by us. . . ."

(Drayton, *Polyolbion,* 1622)

12. Barnacle geese hatching from trees. (From J. Gerard, *An Herball,* 1597, p. 1391.)

Them turn'd to perfect Fowles, when dropping from the tree
Into the Meery Pond, which under them doth lye,
Waxe ripe, and taking wing, away in flockes doe flye;
Which well our Ancients did among our Wonders place.

Which of Drayton's "ancients" he follows here, whether Giraldus, Turner, or another, it is idle to speculate. Du Bartas includes a similar passage (Week 1, Day 6, pp. 228–29):

So, slowe Boötes vnderneath him sees,
In th'ycie *Iles*, those Goslings hatcht of Trees,
Whose fruitfull leaves, falling into the Water,
Are turn'd (they say) to living Fowles soone after.
So, rotten sides of broken Shipps doo change
To *Barnacles*; O Transformation strange!
'Twas first a greene Tree, then a gallant Hull,
Lately a mushrum, now a flying Gull.

Far from abandoning the theory of abiogenesis, science merely leaned to the ship tradition; the phenomenon is frequently discussed—by Turner, Gesner, the herbalist John Gerard, William Harrison, and others.[24]

Equally venerable was the belief in the osprey's magic power over fish, what Shakespeare (*Cor.* IV. vii. 35) calls its "sovereignty of nature," or as Drayton's Holland explains (134–38):

[24] For a full history of both the word *barnacle* and its famous legend, cf. Max Müller, *Lectures on the Science of Language* (2d Ser., New York, 1865), pp. 555–70. The account of Hector Boece, quoted by Müller, is presented by William Harrison in "Description of Scotland" (*Holinshed's Chronicles,* London, 1577, I, pp. 13–14). Further valuable studies are Ray Lankaster, "The History of the Barnacle and the Goose," *Diversions of a Naturalist* (New York, 1915), pp. 117–28; and Edward Heron-Allen, *Barnacles in Nature and Myth* (London, 1928).

The Ospray oft here seene, though seldome here it breeds,
Which over them the Fish no sooner doe espie,
But (betwixt him and them, by an antipathy)
Turning their bellies up, as though their death they saw,
They at his pleasure lye, to stuffe his glutt'nous maw.

This passage closely follows Turner, who further declares that anglers sometimes profit by this secret:

Our anglers smear or mix their bait with Ospray's fat, arguing that thus the bait will prove more efficacious from the fact that, when the Ospray hovers in the air, whatever fishes be below turn up and show their whitish bellies (as it is believed, the nature of the Aquila compelling them to this), that it may choose that one which it prefers.[25]

Caius reports the phenomenon as "opinio apud nostrum vulgus in Britannia."[26] But Aldrovandi explains that the fish are stupefied by a secretion dropped into the water by the osprey.[27] In his use of books, Drayton is at least following the best scientific tradition.

Song XXV concludes with a rejoinder by Lindsey, who, despising the birds of the "foggy Fennes," boasts eleven upland birds, which "more ayrie are, and make fine spirits and blood" (336–50). Here Drayton distinctly relies upon his friend Camden, perhaps also Caius.

Besides the bustard and the "shouler" (shoveler) Dray-

[25] "Piscatores nostrates escis fallendis piscibus destinatis, haliaeeti adipem illinunt, aut immiscent, putantes hoc argumento escam efficaciorem futuram, quod haliaeeto sese in aere librante, pisces quotquot subsunt (natura aquilae ad hoc cogente, ut creditur) sese resupinent, & ventres albicantes, ut quem liberet, eligeret exhibeant." (Evans, *op. cit.*, pp. 36–37.)

[26] *Ibid.*, p. 192.

[27] Cited by Charles E. Raven, *English Naturalists from Neckam to Ray* (London, Cambridge University Press, 1947), p. 143.

ton names the plovers "gray, and greene" (gray or golden plover or lapwing), quail, rail, "puet" (lapwing or black-headed gull), godwit, "stint" (dunlin), and in detail two others:

The *Knot,* that called was *Canutus* Bird of old,
Of that great King of *Danes,* his name that still doth hold,
His apetite to please, that farre and neere was sought,
For him (as some have sayd) from *Denmarke* hither brought
The *Dotterell,* which we thinke a very daintie dish,
Whose taking makes such sport, as man no more can wish;
For as you creepe, or cowre, or lye, or stoupe, or goe,
So marking you (with care) the Apish Bird doth doe,
And acting every thing, doth never marke the Net,
Till he be in the Snare, which men for him have set.[28]

This account, as well as the names of other members in the group, is closely related to a passage in Camden, who for the 1607 edition of *Britannia* adds thus to the natural history of Lincolnshire:

Teal, Quails, Woodcocks, Pheasants, Partridge, Ec. but such as we have no Latin words for, and that are so delicate and agreeable, that the nicest palates always cover them, viz. Puittes, Godwitts, Knotts, that is, as I take it, Canutes's birds, for they are believ'd to fly hither out of Denmark; Dotterells, so call'd from their dotish silliness: for the mimick birds are caught at candlelight by the fowler's gestures; if he stretch out his arm, they imitate him with their wing; if he holds out his leg, they likewise will do the same with theirs; to be short,

[28] Cf. also the "Sottish Dott'rill ignorant and dull" (*The Owle,* 943), and (*To Thomas Coryate,* 1611, *The Works of Michael Drayton,* I, p. 500).
"As men take Dottrels, so hast thou t'an us.
Which as a man his arme or leg doth set,
So this fond Bird will likewise counterfeit. . . ."

whatsoever the fowler does they do after him, till at last they let the net be drawn over them. But I leave these to be observed either by such as delight curiously to dive into the secrets of nature, or that squander away their estates in luxury and epicurism.[29]

Drayton's (and Camden's) etymology of *knot* is of unknown origin. Newton notes that "in the margin [of *Britannia*] the name is spelt 'Cnotts,' and he [Camden] possibly thought it had to do with a well-known story of that king."[30] Whatever the derivation, it persisted until the time of Linnaeus, who named the species *Tringa canutes.* Finally, for the account of the supposed stupidity of the dotterel (*Charadrius morinellus*) Drayton probably depended upon Caius:

It is a mimic. And so, . . . this bird is caught at night by the light of a candle according to the motions of the captor. For if he stretches out an arm, the bird lifts a wing; if he stretches out a leg, it does likewise. In short, whatever part the fowler plays, the bird does the same. So, being intent on the man's actions, it is fooled by the bird-catcher and caught in his net.[31]

Caius accordingly names this bird *Morinellus*—a double pun, from *morus,* "a fool," and *Morini,* an ancient name

[29] *Britannia,* p. 472. Later editors suggest that "D. was perhaps the 'hunter after natures workes' who furnished his friend the antiquary with information about these Lincolnshire birds." (*The Works of Michael Drayton,* V, p. 244.)

[30] Newton, *op. cit.,* p. 498, note 1.

[31] "Imitatrix avis est. Ideo, . . . hec noctu ad lumen candelae pro capientis gestu capitur. Nam si is expandit brachium, extendit & illa alam: si is tibiam, & illa itidem. Breviter quicquid gerit auceps, idem facit & ales. Ita humanis gestibus intenta avis, ab aucipe decipitur, & rhete obvelatur." (Evans, *op. cit.,* pp. 204–205.)

for the people of Flanders, where he had first observed the dotterel.[32] Thus the early history of both knot and dotterel, popularized in Drayton's poetry, is reflected in scientific nomenclature, *canutes* and *morinellus* being the specific designation of these birds.

Unlike the bird chronicles of *Polyolbion,* clearly reminiscent of Du Bartas, Camden, and the scientific authority of Turner, Caius, Belon, and Gesner, *Noahs Flood* (1630) now reflects only Du Bartas for bird names as also for moralizings. Exclusive of birds, Drayton's theme shows familiarity with Pererius' *Commentarium et disputationum in Genesim,* the popular anthology well known to the author of *Paradise Lost.* Milton must have known Drayton's poem; yet except for the fact of their mutual debt to Du Bartas and Pererius, nothing in *Noahs Flood* suggests Milton's account of creation. Where Drayton varies his debt to the French to notice the living habits of birds, Milton, perhaps through Pererius, looks back to the hexaemera.

In regard to Drayton's bird names here (a total of thirty-eight), his editors remark that, though "Drayton's manner of treatment is like Sylvester's, the substance of his descriptions is usually different."[33] In this native interest and accuracy *Noahs Flood* carries on the tradition which reached its height in *Polyolbion:* in other respects this biblical work is merely learned and pedestrian. For present

[32] A diminutive of *dolt.* According to Newton, in 1676 Willughby learned the true meaning of this legend: "Instead of their aping the gestures of the men, it was the men who aped those of the birds, as the latter were being driven into the nets; for, as everyone who has watched the actions of the *Limicolae* must know, it is their common habit as they run to extend a wing and often simultaneously a leg." (Newton, *op. cit.,* p. 161.)

[33] *The Works of Michael Drayton,* V, p. 224.

purposes a few examples will suffice; removed from the catalogue they show to more advantage as observation is combined with commonplace (1391 ff.):

The swift-wing'd Swallow feeding as it flyes,
With the fleet Martlet thrilling throw the Skyes, . . .
The soaring Kyte there scantled his large wings,
And to the Arke the hovering Castrill brings; . . .
The carefull Storke, since Adam wondred at
For thankfulnesse, to those where he doth breed,
That his ag'd Parents naturally doth feed,
In filiall duty as instructing man.

And a marginal note states: "The Storke, used to build upon houses, leaveth ever one behinde him for the owner." Thus easily Drayton lapses into the mood of *The Owle* which binds him to a dead past. In startling contrast are other passages, such as that describing the dove which after the deluge Noah sends forth (856 ff.):

When the glad Bird stayes all the day abroad,
And wondrous proud that he a place had found,
Who of a long time had not toucht the ground,
Drawes in his head, and thrusteth out his breast,
Spreadeth his tayle, and swelleth up his crest,
And turning round and round with Cuttry cooe,
As when the female Pigeon and he wooe;
Bathing himselfe, which long he had not done,
And dryes his feathers in the welcome Sunne,
Pruning his plumage, clensing every quill, . . .

This preoccupation with birds for their own sake leads the poet away from his books, away from his major theme, to direct observation; in this manner *Noahs Flood* repeats sporadically the triumph achieved in *Polyolbion.*

Concentration upon Drayton's birds affords opportunity to observe the evolution of a single facet in the versatile art of this great Elizabethan. From the medieval symbolism in *The Owle,* with its admixture of fable and legend, Drayton advanced through the hybrid *Man in the Moone* to the rare achievements of *Polyolbion.* Here the poet's musty antiquarian journeys are occasionally relieved by accounts of birds most of which obviously he knew directly and all of which he delighted in. Drayton has become a true naturalist completing his observation of nature by resorting also to books. With the anticlimactic *Noahs Flood* his work is concluded. In effect, then, the transition in Drayton's outlook parallels the vastly more gradual growth of the New Science from the bondage of tradition. Between two worlds, Drayton's poetry about birds vividly exemplifies this new approach as it also amply shares the new method. Beside this fact the minor links which have been noted with Chaucer, with Spenser, and with Milton are insignificant.

VI : *Conclusion*

ALTHOUGH THE PRESENT STUDY has not been concerned primarily with the philosophic and religious impact of science upon poetry, as in the recent survey by Douglas Bush, in the last analysis any study of birds in literature bears more directly upon man than upon birds. Through the centuries, through millions of years, the life of birds has continued unchanged. Allowing for the processes of evolution, the appearance of birds, their habits, and their songs have varied less than the contours of a landscape. Perennially a part of nature's cycle, bird life is still the same—except in the eyes of humankind. This incidental relationship has constantly varied its complexion as men of different ages have sought to fit all nature into their pattern of beliefs. As Wordsworth knew, these human impressions are half-created, half-perceived. So it is that man's created bird myths reflect his own varying ideals through the centuries until in a new age subjective fictions are replaced by verifiable facts.

In so far as the encyclopedists and other early naturalists confined their activity to books, natural history remained word study, philology, and an agent of moral guidance. Yet all the while there were hosts of laymen—hunters or mere outdoor folk—who without books learned well the lore of the field through an innate, responsive awareness. In time a small group came to regard books and field as companions, neither complete without the other and each necessary to the other. By and large, the history of ornithology, as of the other sciences, is marked by the gradual awakening to the importance of this double aim. With the eclipse of the scientific Aristotle, the Western world required some two thousand years to reach the fringes of this idea. When William Turner, the student, left his books for the field to verify or amend ancient authority, in England the tide had definitely turned.

To what extent was this changing picture reflected in contemporary poetry? In the restricted areas of bird lore and with a narrow circle of four poets, the preceding chapters have provided a tentative answer to this question.

With differences, Chaucer, Spenser, and Milton adhered to the notion that birds exist as symbols of good and evil. Though of this group Chaucer was closest to the objective attitude of later centuries, the poetry of all three joined in perpetuating the outlook of the still-popular encyclopedias. Spenser's friend Sidney believed that poetry and nature bore the same relationship as Bartholomew had declared for the Platonic worlds of spirit and flesh. To this poetic creed Milton also implicitly subscribed, despite the early promise of the new attitude more expressive of seventeenth-century thinking. This Drayton alone carried over into his poetry, although his early effort is largely in the older tradition. Drayton's triumph lies in the revelation that poetry is capable of serving a new end in objective and intimate descriptions of bird life. In this art Drayton is remote from his contemporaries; he is much nearer Chaucer, who had divorced nature from morality, and he anticipates John Clare, the great nineteenth-century nature poet. With the true romantics, birds were destined again to return as symbols, but more intimately than ever they were to evoke human mood and to pronounce man's humble place in the scheme of nature.

Index to Birds

Named by Chaucer, Spenser, Milton, and Drayton

THE FOLLOWING INDEX discloses that Chaucer names roughly 51 different bird species, Spenser 44, Milton 32, and Drayton 94. Spenser's and Milton's bat, like Drayton's roc, is omitted from this count, but Spenser's whistler, night raven, and tedula are treated as distinct species. Drayton's two plovers, "gray, and greene," either gray or golden plover and lapwing, are counted as one, for elsewhere in his verse appear "lapwing" and "puet," also a name for the black-headed gull. The "sea-meaw," one of the gulls—possibly again the black-headed—is considered distinct from the "seagull," because to Spenser and Drayton the two birds seemed to be different kinds. With the vague designations of classical writers on the one hand, and the strong family resemblances of birds on the other, it is small wonder that men who lived before Linnaeus fumbled with names. Hence no exact figure of bird totals can be arrived at.

Both Chaucer and Spenser were intimately familiar with falconry. Chaucer names goshawk (the female usually termed *falcon*), peregrine, merlin, sparrow hawk, and buzzard; Spenser names only goshawk and kestrel, though his verse indicates extensive knowledge. Milton has a single allusion to "a hawk"; and Drayton mentions goshawk, hen harrier ("ring-tail"), kestrel, sparrow hawk, buzzard, and osprey ("bald buzzard"). Only Drayton knew the duck kinds, a total of eight. Of the owls there is little to indicate species. Spenser's "strich" may denote the screech or barn owl as distinct from the "litch owl" of Drayton, who elsewhere seems to allude to the tawny owl. But if "litch" is equivalent to Turner's "lyke," then the European eagle owl (*Bubo*) is meant. As the common omen, "owl" probably referred mostly to the tawny owl, whose note "too whit too whoo" was celebrated by Drayton and Shakespeare. And of course the little owl has been only recently introduced in England.

Of the huge family of finches, buntings, and sparrows, Chaucer names bullfinch ("alp"), goldfinch, hedge sparrow ("heysog"), and the unidentified "terin," and he alludes to both finches and sparrows. Spenser mentions sparrows only; Milton finch and sparrow; and Drayton goldfinch and yellowhammer, as also the general terms sparrow and finch—names universal, even today, for all little, undistinguished birds. In addition to the word "dove" Chaucer names wood dove and, from Ovid, culver (Lat. *columba*), the latter being applied indiscriminately to stock dove, rock dove, and wood dove. Spenser names culver and turtledove; Milton turtledove only; and Drayton turtledove and wood dove. So of the four British doves only turtledoves and wood doves find a name, the culver remaining vague. Like the others, Chaucer knew chiefly the common skylark ("lark" or "laverock"); the "chalaundre," an Anglicism for *chelaundre* (the calandra lark of southern Europe) named in the *Romaunt.* Drayton alone knew the wood lark, less common and rarely beautiful in song as in flight. Distinction was seldom indicated between mavis and mistle thrush. Possibly Spenser knew the latter as "thrush" as distinct from mavis and blackbird (ouzel), though the songs of the three birds are somewhat alike. Drayton distinguished blackbird from mavis but seems to have been unfamiliar with mistle thrush.

The few allusions to ouzel and the many to mavis, throstle, and throstle cock may imply that the varied warbling of the blackbird was often attributed to the song thrush. Just as any small grayish bird would likely be called a sparrow, so the songbirds, loud but usually unseen, were not often distinguished.

Of the four poets Drayton alone deliberately chose to versify birds from observation and from reading. His total number, vastly more than those of the other poets, brings into question the extent of his actual outdoor observations. But, as has been pointed out, Drayton's claims to distinction as a poet of birds rest, not upon numbers, but rather upon the accuracy and intimacy of his art.

The Index presents bird names first as they appear in the poetry, these names occasionally applying to more than one species. Then follow the common modern names as they appear in Alfred Newton's *A Dictionary of Birds,* Charles Swainson's *Provincial Names and Folk Lore of British Birds,* and H. Kirke Swann's *A Dictionary of English and Folk-Names of British Birds.* The fairly complete lists of allusions to birds (singular and plural) which follow are based upon *The Concordance to Chaucer* (Tatlock and Kennedy), *The Concordance to Spenser* (Osgood), *A Subject Index to the Poems of Edmund Spenser* (Whitman), and *An Index to the*

Columbia Edition of Milton (Patterson). The birds of Drayton have been listed from four poems: *The Owle, The Man in the Moone, Polyolbion,* and *Noahs Flood* (it is unlikely that his other poems include bird names absent from these four). Occasional quotation is included to exemplify the poets' manner. The page numbers which occasionally appear at the end of entries refer to discussion in the text. In the Index poem titles have been modernized.

Abbreviations Used in Index

Chaucer

Anel.	*Complaint of Fair Anelida and False Arcite*
B.D.	*Book of the Duchess*
Cl.	*Clerk's Tale*
Co.	*Cook's Tale*
C.Y.	*Canon's Yeoman's Tale*
Fkl.	*Franklin's Tale*
Fri.	*Friar's Tale*
H.F.	*House of Fame*
Kn.	*Knight's Tale*
L.G.W.	*Legend of Good Women*
Mch.	*Merchant's Tale*
Mcp.	*Manciple's Tale*
Mel.	*Tale of Melibeus*
Mil.	*Miller's Tale*
Mk.	*Monk's Tale*
M.L.	*Man of Law's Tale*
Np.	*Nun's Priest's Tale*
Pard.	*Pardoner's Tale*
P.F.	*Parliament of Fowls*
Prol.	*Prologue to the Canterbury Tales*
R.R.	*Romaunt of the Rose*

Rv.	*Reeve's Tale*
Sh.	*Shipman's Tale*
Sq.	*Squire's Tale*
Sum.	*Summoner's Tale*
Th.	*Tale of Sir Thopas*
T.C.	*Troilus and Criseyde*
W.B.	*Wife of Bath's Tale*

Spenser

Am.	*Amoretti*
As.	*Astrophel*
Col.	*Colin Clout's Come Home Again*
D.	*Daphnaida*
Ded. Son.	*Verses Addressed by the Author of the Fairy Queen to Various Noblemen*
Epith.	*Epithalamion*
F.Q.	*Fairy Queen*
Gn.	*Vergil's Gnat*
H.H.B.	*Hymn of Heavenly Beauty*
H.L.	*Hymn in Honor of Love*
Hub.	*Mother Hubbard's Tale*
Mui.	*Muiopotmos*
Pet.	*Visions of Petrarch*
Proth.	*Prothalamion*
Ro.	*Ruins of Rome*
Ti.	*Ruins of Time*
S.C.	*Shepherd's Calendar*
T.M.	*Tears of the Muses*
Van.	*Visions of the World's Vanity*

Milton

A.	*Animadversions*
A.P.	*Apology against a Pamphlet*

Ar.	*Areopagitica*
B.	*History of Britain*
B.N.	*Brief Notes upon a Late Sermon*
C.	*Colasterion*
C.B.	*Commonplace Book*
C.D.	*Christian Doctrine*
C.E.	*Carmina Elegiaca*
C.G.	*Reason of Church Government Urg'd against Prelaty*
Co.	*Comus*
1D.	*First Defense*
D.	*Doctrine and Discipline of Divorce*
E.D.	*Epitaphium Damonis*
El.	*Elegy*
H.M.	*History of Muscovia*
I.P.	*Il Penseroso*
K.	*Eikonoklastes*
L'A.	*L'Allegro*
Mar.	*Marginalia*
M.M.C.	*Correspondence of Milton and Mylius*
N.	*On the Morning of Christ's Nativity*
nm.	non-Miltonic (quoted)
P.L.	*Paradise Lost*
P.R.	*Paradise Regained*
Pro.	*Prolusions*
R.	*Of Reformation*
So.	*Sonnets*
Su.	*Supplement of Alexander More*
S.D.	*Pro Se Defensio*
S.A.	*Samson Agonistes*
2D.	*Second Defense*
T.	*Tetrachordon*
Note:	The roman numerals refer to book, chapter, or order of works bearing the same title, as the Prolusions and First

and Second Defenses; the arabics refer to lines. Citations in parentheses denote volume and page in the Columbia edition.

Drayton

M.M.	*The Man in the Moon*
N.F.	*Noah's Flood*
O.	*The Owl*
Po.	*Polyolbion*

Index to Birds Named by Chaucer, Spenser, Milton, and Drayton

ALCATRAS (man-of-war, pelican, and other birds. See Newton, p. 6).

Drayton: O. 549 ff. ("[The pelican is] Most like to that sharpe-sighted *A*,/that beates the Aire above the liquid Glasse:/The New-Worlds Bird").

ALP (bullfinch).

Chaucer: R.R. 658.

Drayton: Po. XIII. 74 ("Nope"). See p. 33.

ARCHANGEL (finch? tit?).

Chaucer: R.R. 915. See p. 34.

AUK (razorbill).

Drayton: Po. XXVIII. 499 ff. ("The Mullett, and the *A* . . ./ Birds of the strangest kind. . . ."). See pp. 121–22.

BALD BUZZARD ("Properly the Marsh-Harrier, but also applied to the Osprey"—Swann).

Drayton: O. 865.

BARNACLE (brant [brent], barnacle goose).

Drayton: Po. XXV. 113; Po. XXVII. 304 ("Tree-geese Call'd *B*"). See pp. 123–25.

BAT.

Spenser: F.Q. ii. xii. 36. 6 ("lether-winged *b,* dayes enimy").

Milton: K. 15 nm (V, p. 219) ("owls, *b,* and such fatal birds"); M.M.C. 53 nm (XII, p. 357) ("do we lament shrilly with *b*").

Drayton: O. 502 ("the black-ey'd *B*"), 518.

BIDCOCK (bilcock, water rail).

Drayton: Po. XXV. 100.

BITTERN.

Chaucer: W.B. 972 ("as a *b* bombleth in the myre").

Spenser: F.Q. ii. viii. 50. 2 ("as a *B* in the Eagles clawe").

Milton: 1D. v. (VII, p. 281) ("lay snares for your own *b*").

Drayton: O. 921, Po. XXV. 103 ("Buzzing *b*"). See p. 120.

BUNTING. See Finch.

Drayton: O. 380, 1058; Po. XIII. 74.

BUSTARD.

Drayton: Po. XXV. 351 ff. ("big-boan'd *B,* whose body beares that size,/That he against the wind must runne, e're he can rise").

BUZZARD. See Hawk.

Chaucer: R.R. 4033.

Milton: K. 1 (V, p. 87).

Drayton: O. 184, 204, 387.

CHALAUNDRE (calandra lark).

Chaucer: R.R. 81, 663, 914.

CHOUGH (jackdaw, a former usage). See Crow.

Chaucer: P.F. 345 ("the theef the *c*"); W.B. 232 ("cow").

Drayton: O. 188, 893, 913.

COCK.

Chaucer: Mil. 3687; Np. *passim;* P.F. 350 ("*c,* that orloge is of thorpes lyte"), 357; Prol. 823; T.C. iii. 1415.

Spenser: F.Q. iv. v. 41. 8; S.C. Sept. 46 ("as *c* on his dunghill crowing cranck").

Milton: C.E. 1.3 (I, p. 326); Co. 345 (I, p. 98); 1D. 5 (VII, p. 281); L'A. 49 (I, p. 36), 114 (I, p. 38); P.L. vii. 443 (II, p. 227); Pro. i. (XII, p. 125, 137); Pro. v. (XII, p. 197).

Drayton: N.F. 387; O. 72.

HEN.

Chaucer: Np. *passim;* Prol. 177; R.R. 6856; W.B. 1112.

Milton: B.ii. (X, p. 50).

Drayton: N.F. 389, 895; O. 66, 1281.

COOT.

Drayton: O. 941; Po. XXV. 69 ff. See p. 120.

CORMORANT.

Chaucer: P.F. 362 ("hote *c* of glotenye").

Spenser: F.Q. ii. xii. 8. 5 ("*C,* with birds of ravenous race").

Milton: P.L. iv. 196 (II, p. 113) ("[Satan] sat like a *c*").

Drayton: N.F. 437; O. 351, 377; Po. XXV. 127 ff.

CRANE.

Chaucer: P.F. 344 ("*c* the geaunt, with his trompes soune").

Spenser: F.Q. 1. iv. 21. 5 ("like a *c* his necke was long and fyne"); F.Q. vi. vii. 42. 5 ("stalking stately, like a *c*").

Milton: B.N. (VI, p. 157); P.L. i. 576 (II, p. 29); P.L. vii. 430 (II, p. 227) ("prudent *c* so steers her voyage"); Pro. vi. (XII, p. 237) ("Jupiter sent them *c;* fable says stork"); Pro. vii. (XII, p. 283).

Drayton: N.F. 378; O. 75, 755; Po. XXV. 93 ("the stately *c*").

CROW (carrion crow. The family *Corvidae* includes also chough, daw, jay, pie, raven, and rook.).

Chaucer: Kn. 2692; Mcp. *passim;* P.F. 345, 363 ("*c,* with vois of care").

Spenser: S.C. Mar. 110 ("a fowling net,/Which he for carrion *c* had set"); S.C. Dec. 136.

Milton: Ar. (IV, p. 314); B.4 (X, p. 191) ("frays of dukes

CROW—*Continued.*
no more worth recording than wars of kites or *c*"); Pro. vi. (XII, p. 239).
Drayton: N.F. 404, 893; O. *passim.*

CUCKOO.
Chaucer: Kn. 1810, 1930; P.F. 358 ("*c* ever unkynde"), 498, 505, 603, 612 ("mortherere of the heysoge").
Spenser: Am. XIX. 1 ("Merry *c* the messenger of spring"); Am. LXXXIV. 3.
Milton: 1D. v. (VII, p. 343); 1D. v. (VII, p. 347); K. 16 (V, p. 224) ("constancy in *c* to be always in same liturgy"); So. I. 6 (I, p. 47) ("the shallow *c*'s bill"); So. I. 9 (I, p. 47); So. XII. 4 (I, p. 62). See pp. 85–87.
Drayton: O. 927, 983 ("Th' Italians call him Becco [of a Nod]"), *passim.*

CULVER (wood dove? rock dove? stock dove?).
Chaucer: L.G.W. 2319.
Spenser: Am. LXXXVIII. 1; F.Q. ii. vii. 34. 6; F.Q. iii. vii. 39. 2 ("in foote doth beare/A trembling *C*"); T.M. 246 (wofull *C*"). See Dove.

CURLEW.
Drayton: M.M. 206 ("*c* scratching in the Oose and Ore.").

DAW (jackdaw).
Spenser: Hub. 913.
Milton: S.D. (IX, p. 201); S.D. (IX, p. 269).
Drayton: O. 188, 893, 913. See Crow.

DIVEDOPPER (divedapper, dabchick, little grebe).
Drayton: M.M. 188; Po. XXV. 76 ff. ("Now up, now downe againe, that hard it is to proove,/Whether under water most it liveth, or above").

DOTTEREL.
Drayton: O. 943 ("the Sottish *D;* ignorant and dull"); Po. XXV. 345 ff. See pp. 127–29.

DOVE (the family *Columbidae* includes turtledove, rock dove, wood dove, and stock dove).

Chaucer: B.D. 250; H.F. i. 137; Kn. 1962; Mch. 2139; Pard. 397 ("as dooth a *d* sittynge on a berne"); P.F. 237, 341; R.R. 1219, 1298; T.C. iii. 1496.

Spenser: Am. LXXXVIII. 8; Ded. Son. vi. 9; Epith. 358; F.Q. iii. iv. 49. 4; F.Q. iii. vi. 11. 4 ("fled as flit as ayery *D*"); F.Q. iv. Pr. 5. 2 ("Venus dearling *d*"); F.Q. iv. viii. 11. 1; F.Q. iv. viii. 31. 2; F.Q. v. xii. 5. 9; F.Q. vi. viii. 49. 9; Mui. 291; T.M. 402 ("prune his plumes like ruffed *d*").

Milton: B. iv. (X, p. 194); C.D. i. 6 (XIV, p. 367) ("likeness of *d* seems representation of ineffable affection of Father for Son"); C.D. i. 6 (XIV, p. 371); P.L. i. 21 (II, p. 9) ("*d*-like satst brooding"); P.L. xi. 857 (II, p. 376); P.R. i. 30 (II, p. 406); P.R. i. 83 (II, p. 408); P.R. i. 282 (II, p. 415) ("Spirit descended like a *d*"); 2D. (VIII, p. 237).

Drayton: N.F. 423, 842, 852, 862 ("Pigeon"), 937; O. 903 ("*d* without a gall").

DUCK.

Chaucer: Mil. 3576 ("as dooth the white *d* after hir drake"); N.P. 4580; P.F. 498, 589.

Spenser: F.Q. v. ii. 54. 2 ("Flowne at a flush of *d* foreby a brooke").

Milton: H.M. i (X, p. 333).

Drayton: M.M. 184; Po. XXV. 53 ff. ("The *D,* and Mallard first, the Falconers onely sport, . . ./Their numbers be so great, the waters covering quite,/That rais'd, the spacious ayre is darkened with their flight"). (Drayton names goldeneye, goosander, mallard, sheldrake, shoveller, pochard, teal, and wigeon.)

DRAKE.

Chaucer: L.G.W. 2450; Mil. 3576; P.F. 360.

EAGLE.

Chaucer: H.F. i. 499, 501, 507; H.F. ii. 21, 483; H.F. iii. 20, 900; Kn. 2178; L.G.W. 2319; Mk. 3365, 3573; P.F. 330, 332, 373, 393 ("the tercel *e,* as that ye knowen wel"), 449, 463, 540, 646; Sq. 123; T.C. ii. 926; T.C. iii. 1496. (Chaucer often uses "tercel" and "tercelet" of the male *e* and male goshawk, "formel" of the female *e.* See Falcon.)

Spenser: F.Q. i. viii. 48. 6; F.Q. i. x. 47. 6; F.Q. i. xi. 9. 5; F.Q. i. xi. 34. 3; F.Q. ii. viii. 50. 2; F.Q. ii. ix. 50. 9; F.Q. ii. x. 70. 9; F.Q. iii. vii. 39. 3; F.Q. iii, xi. 34. 1; F.Q. iv. vii. 18. 6; F.Q. v. iv. 42. 1; F.Q. v. xi. 24. 7; F.Q. v. xii. 5. 9; H.H.B. 138; H.L. 69; Ro. 17. 10, 18. 10; S.C. Jan. 222; Van. 4. 6.

Milton: Ar. (IV, p. 344); M.A.R. (XVIII, p. 282); P.L. v. 271 (II, p. 153); P.L. vii. 423 (II, p. 226); P.L. xi. 185 (II, p. 352); S.A. 1695 (I, p. 397); S.D. (IX, p. 67).

Drayton: N.F. 363; O. 193 *passim.*

ESTRIDGE. See Ostrich.

FALCON (goshawk, female).

Chaucer: L.G.W. 1120; P.F. 337, 529 ("the tercelet of the *f,* to diffyne"); R.R. 546; Sq. 411 *passim;* T.C. iii. 1784; T.C. iv. 413.

Spenser: F.Q. ii. vii. 34. 6; F.Q. ii. xi. 36. 6; F.Q. iii. xi. 39. 8; F.Q. iv. viii. 31. 2; F.Q. v. ii. 54. 1; F.Q. v. v. 15.2; F.Q. vi. viii. 49. 9; F.Q. vi. vii. 9. 1 ("a cast of *f*"); H.H.B. 26 ("soare *f*"); Ti. 128.

Drayton: N.F. 423, 425; O. 207, 390; Po. XXV. 53.

FIELDFARE.

Chaucer: P.F. 364 ("frosty *f*"); R.R. 5510; T.C. iii. 861.

FINCH (family *Fringillidae* includes finches, buntings, and sparrows). See Goldfinch.

Chaucer: Prol. 652; R.R. 658, 915.

Milton: Pro. vii. (XII, p. 277).

HAWK—*Continued.*

Milton: C.G. i. 1 (III, p. 187).

(See also Goshawk, Peregrine, Kestrel, Sparrow-hawk, Merlin, Ringtail, Buzzard, and Osprey.)

HECCO (green woodpecker).

Drayton: O. 191, 206; Po. XIII. 80 ("laughing *h*").

HEDGE SPARROW (heysog, dunnock).

Chaucer: P.F. 612 ("heysoge").

Drayton: O. 697 ["hedge-sparrow and her Compeere the Wren/(Which simple people call our Ladies-Hen")], 1015.

HERON.

Chaucer: Fkl. 1197; P.F. 346 ("the eles foo, the *h*"); Sq. 68 ("heronsewe").

Spenser: F.Q. ii. xi. 43. 2; F.Q. iv. iii. 19. 3; F.Q. vi. vii. 9. 2 ("an Herneshaw, that lyes aloft on wing").

Drayton: M.M. 203; N.F. 439; O. 71; Po. XXV. 94.

HOOPOE.

Milton: S.D. (IX, p. 203) ("[More left] not a phoenix but a fowl-feeding hoopoe").

IBIS.

Drayton: O. 645 ("a destroyer of the Locust, Plinie"—marginal note).

ILKE. See Swan.

JAY.

Chaucer: C.Y. 1397; Mcp. 132 ("men teche a *j*"); M.L. 774; P.F. 346 ("scornynge *j*"); Prol. 642; Rv. 4154.

Spenser: F.Q. ii. viii. 5. 8.

Drayton: O. 595 ("jetting *j*"), 603 ("jolly *j*"), 663 ("carion *J*"); Po. XIII. 80 ("counterfetting *j*").

KESTREL.

Spenser: F.Q. ii. iii. 4. 4 ("his *k* kynd/A pleasing vaine of glory").

Drayton: N.F. 402 ("hovering Castrell"); O. 821.
KINGFISHER.
Drayton: M.M. 200 ff. See p. 115.
HALCYON.
Milton: N. 68 (I, p. 4).
Drayton: N.F. 441.
KITE (puttock).
Chaucer: Kn. 1179, P.F. 349; Sq. 624, 625, 628.
Spenser: F.Q. ii. viii. 16. 9; F.Q. ii. xi. 11. 5 ("puttock"); F.Q. v. v. 15. 1, 5; F.Q. v. xii. 30. 3; F.Q. vi. viii. 28. 4 ("foolish *k*").
Milton: B.4 (X, p. 191); E.D. 103 (I, p. 306).
Drayton: N.F. 401; O. 73, 184, 201, *passim.*
KNOT.
Drayton: Po. XXV. 341. See pp. 127–28.
LAPWING (puet, green plover).
Chaucer: P.F. 347 ("false *l*, ful of trecherye").
Spenser: Gn. 405.
Drayton: O. 946 ("squealing *l*"); Po. XXV. 339 ("Puet").
LARK (laverock, skylark. See also Chalaundre and Wood Lark.).
Chaucer: H.F. ii. 38 ("as lightly as I were a *l*"); Kn. 1491 ("bisy *l*, messanger of day"), 2210, 2212; L.G.W. 141; P.F. 340; R.R. 662 ("Laverokkes"), 915; T.C. iii. 1191.
Spenser: As. 33; Epith. 80 ("merry *l* hir mattins sings aloft"); F.Q. i. i. 44. 7; F.Q. i. xi. 51. 9; F.Q. ii. vi. 3. 3; F.Q. vii. vi. 47. 5 ("Like darred *l*, not daring up to looke"); S.C. June 51; S.C. Nov. 71.
Milton: C.E. i. 8 (I, p. 326); Co. 316 (I, p. 97) ("low roosted *l*"); L'A. 41 (I, p. 36) ("to hear the *l* begin his flight"); P.R. ii. 279 (II, p. 434); Pro. ii. (XII, p. 153).
Drayton: N.F. 397 ("ayry *l* his *Haleluiah* sung"); O. 133, 217, 383.

LINNET.

Drayton: O. 109, 217; Po. XIII. 72.

LITCH OWL (eagle owl, "lyke foule"—Turner).

Drayton: O. 302.

MALLARD (wild duke, male).

Drayton: M.M. 185; O. 945 ("lecherous *m*"); Po. XXV. 53 ff. See Duck.

MARTLET (house martin).

Drayton: N.F. 392 ("fleet Martlet thrilling throw the Skyes"); O. 83.

MAVIS (throstle, mistle thrush).

Chaucer: P.F. 364 ("throstel old"); R.R. 619, 665; Th. 1959 ("thrustelcok made eek hir lay"), 1963.

Spenser: Am. LXXXIV. 3; Epith. 81 ("The thrush [mistle *t*] replyes; the Mavis [song *t*] descant playes"); F.Q. vi. iv. 17. 3 ("To take the ayre and heare the thrushes song").

Drayton: N.F. 417 ("Merle and *M*"); O. 114, 220 ("warbling Throstle Cocke"), 1133 ("warbling *m*"), 1259 ("the jocund throstle, for his varying note/Clad by the Eagle in a speckled Cote"); Po. XIII. 55 ("throstell with shrill sharps"). (For confusion of two birds, see p. 81, n. 23.)

MERLE (ouzel, blackbird).

Spenser: Epith. 82 ("The Ouzell shrills; the Ruddock warbles soft").

Drayton: N.F. 417, 896; O. 114 ("the sweet *M*, and warbling Mavis"), 221 ("ousell"); Po. XIII. 58 ("The Woosell near at hand, that hath a golden bill, . . . the *M*").

MERLIN.

Chaucer: P.F. 339, 611. See Hawk.

MEW. See Sea Meaw.

MORECOOT. See Water Hen.

MULLET. See Puffin.

OSTRICH—*Continued.*

Drayton: N.F. 385 ("Iron-eating Estridge, whose bare Thyes /Resembling mans. . . ."); O. 389; Po. XXII. 238.

OUZEL. See Merle.

OWL (tawny—brown—owl?).

Chaucer: L.G.W. 2253; N.P. 4282; P.F. 343 ("the *o* eek, that of deth the bode bryngeth"), 599; Sq. 648; T.C. v. 319, 382; W.B. 1081.

Spenser: F.Q. i. v. 30. 6; F.Q. i. ix. 33. 6; F.Q. ii. vii. 23. 3; F.Q. ii. ix. 50. 9; F.Q. ii. xi. 8. 3; F.Q. ii. xii. 36. 4 ("ill-faste *O*"); F.Q. iv. 5. 41. 8; S.C. June 24; S.C. Dec. 72.

Milton: C.B. (XVIII, p. 138); K. 15 nm (V, p. 219) ("*o,* bats, and such fatal birds"); Pro. i. (XII, p. 145); So. XII. 4 (I, p. 62) ("*o* and cuckoos, asses, apes, and dogs").

Drayton: N.F. 432, 903 ("*o* cryes Too whit too Whoo"); O. 103 ("Ascallaphus in Bubonem," margin), *passim.* See also Shriek Owl and Litch Owl.

PARROT (popinjay, green woodpecker).

Chaucer: Mch. 2322; P.F. 359 ("*p,* ful of delicasye"); R.R. 81, 913; Sh. 1559 ("murie as a papejay"); Th. 1957.

Milton: Pro. vi. (XII, p. 235); 2D. (VIII, p. 55).

Drayton: N.F. 421 ("prating p"), 901; O. 353 *passim.* See p. 33.

PARTRIDGE.

Chaucer: H.F. iii. 302; Prol. 349 ("many a fat *p* hadde he in muwe").

Spenser: F.Q. iii. viii. 33. 3.

Drayton: N.F. 427, 894.

PAVONE. See Peacock.

PEACOCK.

Chaucer: P.F. 356 ("the *p* with his aungels fethres bright"); Prol. 104; Rv. 3926 ("as eny *p* he was proud and gay"); T.C. i. 210.

POOL SNIPE (redshank).
Drayton: Po. XXV. 100.
POPINJAY. See Parrot.
PUET. See Lapwing and Sea Meaw.
PUFFIN (mullet).
Drayton: Po. XXV. 81 ("[*p*] more doth love the brack"); Po. XXVIII. 499 ("mullett").
PUTTOCK. (Also common name for Buzzard and Marsh Harrier. —Swann.). See Kite.
QUAIL.
Chaucer: Cl. 1206; P.F. 339; R.R. 7259.
Drayton: O. 921; Po. XXV. 337 ("corne-land-loving *Q*").
RAIL.
Drayton: Po. XXV. 338.
RAVEN.
Chaucer: H.F. ii. 496; Kn. 2144; P.F. 363 ("*r* wys"); T.C. v. 382 ("as *r*'s qualm").
Spenser: F.Q. ii. viii. 16. 9 ("entombed in the *r* or the Kight"); S.C. Dec. 32 ("to dislodge the *r* of her nest").
Milton: A. 17 (III, p. 172); P.L. xi. 855 (II, p. 376); P.R. ii. 267 (II, p. 433) ("*r* with their horny beaks").
Drayton: N.F. 403, 841, 893; O. 185.
RED SPARROW (reed sparrow, reed bunting).
Drayton: Po. XIII. 74. See Finch.
RING DOVE. See Wood Dove.
RINGTAIL (hen harrier, female).
Drayton: O. 876, 881, 889.
ROBIN. See Ruddock.
ROOK.
Chaucer: H.F. iii. 426.
Spenser: F.Q. ii. xi. 22. 3.
Milton: R. ii. (III, 56).

Drayton: O. 819, 846, 946 ("the ridiculous *r*").
RUCKE (roc).
Drayton: *Battaile of Agincourt* 372 ("An Indian Bird so great, that she is able to carry an Elephant"—margin); N.F. 448. (See Newton, pp. 791 ff.)
RUDDOCK (robin, redbreast).
Chaucer: P.F. 349 ("tame *r*").
Spenser: Epith. 82.
Drayton: N.F. 445; O. 88 ("Red-brest teacheth Charitie"); O. 137 ("Robinet"); O. 711 ("Robin"), 718, *passim;* Po. XIII. 74.
SEAGULL ("A se cob or a see-gell."—Turner).
Spenser: F.Q. ii. xii. 8. 4 ("yelling meaws, with *s* hoars and bace").
Milton: A.P. (III, p. 310) ("pluming and footing this *s*"); C. (IV, p. 248).
Drayton: O. 944.
SEA MEAW (black-headed gull; "fulica . . . a white semaw, with a black cop."—Turner).
Spenser: F.Q. ii. xii. 8. 4 ("yelling meaws, with Sea-gulls hoars and bace").
Drayton: M.M. 183 ("greedy Sea-maw fishing for the fry"); Po. XXV. 123 ("the Sea-meaw, Sea-pye, Gull, and Curlew"). See Puet.
SEA PIE (oystercatcher).
Drayton: Po. XXV. 223.
SHELL FOWL (sheldrake; "Bergander"—Turner).
Drayton: M.M. 184. See Duck.
SHOVELER (spoonbill?).
Drayton: Po. XXV. 353. See Duck.
SHRIEK OWL (barn—screech—owl).
Spenser: Epith. 345 ("let not the *s*, nor the stork be heard");

SHRIEK OWL—*Continued.*

F.Q. ii. xii. 36. 7 ("the rueful strich still waiting on the bere"); T.M. 283 ("fowle goblins and *s*"). See pp. 63–65.

SMEATH (pochard, wigeon).

Drayton: Po. XXV. 67. See Duck.

SNITE (snipe).

Drayton: M.M. 205 ("bidling *s*"); N.F. 440; O. 947; Po. XXV. 99 ("pallat-pleasing *s*").

SPARROW.

Chaucer: P.F. 351 ("*s* Venus sone"); Prol. 626; Sum. 1804 ("chirketh as a *s*").

Spenser: F.Q. vi. ix. 40. 2 ("litle *s* stolen from their nest").

Milton: A. 4 (III, p. 140); E.D. 101 (I, p. 306 ("*s* chooses one mate").

Drayton: O. 137, 369.

SPARROW HAWK.

Chaucer: N.P. 4647 ("he loketh as a *s* with his eyen"); P.F. 338 ("the hardy *s* eke"), 569; R.R. 4033; T.C. iii. 1192; Th. 1957.

Drayton: N.F. 427.

STARLING.

Drayton: O. 634 ("a *s*, that is taught to prate").

STINT (dunlin).

Drayton: Po. XXV. 339.

STORK.

Chaucer: P.F. 361 ("*s* the wreker of avouterye").

Spenser: Epith. 345.

Milton: B.N. (VI, p. 157) ("fable says the crane was a *s*"); B.N. (VI, p. 158) ("[king as] *s* ever pecking at and devouring subjects"); P.L. vii. 423 (II, p. 226).

Drayton: N.F. 406 ("carefull *s*. . . . In filiall duty as instructing man"); O. 912.

TITMOUSE—*Continued.*

Drayton: O. 115, 925.

TROCHYLE (trochilus, a plover).

Drayton: O. 411 ("the base *T* . . . scowre vile Carion for a savoury gayne").

TEDULA.

Spenser: Van. 3. 7. See p. 65, n. 12.

TURKEY COCK.

Drayton: O. 996.

TURTLE (turtledove).

Chaucer: Mch. 2080, 2139; Mil. 3706; P.F. 355 ("wedded *t*, with hire herte trewe"), 510, 577, 583; R.R. 662.

Spenser: As. 178 ("followed her make like *t* chaste"); Col. 340, 865, F.Q. iii. xi. 2. 9; F.Q. iv. viii. 3. 2; F.Q. vi. viii. 33. 6; S.C. Nov. 138 ("*t* on the bared braunch").

Milton: N. 50 (I, p. 3) ("with *t* wing").

Drayton: N.F. 413; O. 65 ("prettie *t*, and the kissing Dove"), 451.

VULTURE.

Chaucer: *Boece* iii. m. 12. 1130–35 ("The foul that highte *v*, . . ."); T.C. i. 788.

Spenser: Epith. 348 ("griesly *v*"); F.Q. i. v. 35. 6; F.Q. iv. iii. 19. 1.

Milton: A.P. (III, pp. 360, 361); K. 9 (V, p. 155); P.L. iii. 431 (II, p. 92); Pro. iii. (XII, p. 165).

Drayton: N.F. 429; O. 350, 443, *passim.*

WAGTAIL.

Drayton: O. 926.

WARYANGLE (shrike).

Chaucer: Fri. 1408 ("as ful of venym been thise *w*"). See p. 34, n. 3.

WATER HEN (gallinule, moorhen).

Drayton: M.M. 186 ("Morecoot"); Po. XXV. 70 ("water-hen"). See p. 120.

WATER OUZEL (dipper, "watercraw"—Turner).
Drayton: Po. XXV. 72 ("Water-woosell next, all over black as Jeat,/With various colours, black, greene, blew, red, russet, white" [!]).
WHISTLER (curlew).
Spenser: F.Q. ii. xii. 36. 8 ("*w* shrill, that who so heares doth dy"). See p. 65, n. 12.
WIGEON.
Drayton: Po. XXV. 67. See p. 119.
WODEWALE (green woodpecker and golden oriole).
Chaucer: R.R. 658, 914. See p. 33.
WOODCOCK.
Milton: C (IV, p. 270) ("this incogitant *w*").
Drayton: O. 600, 947 ("witlesse *w*").
WOOD DOVE (ring dove).
Chaucer: Th. 1960.
Drayton: O. 1051 ("ring-dove").
WOOD LARK.
Drayton: Po. XIII. 73.
WOOSELL. See Ouzel.
WREN.
Drayton: N.F. 448; O. 697, 705; Po. XIII. 74.
YELLOW PATE (yellowhammer).
Drayton: Po. XIII. 75.